BUSINESS

Nokia WAY

SECRETS of the World's Fastest Moving Company

TREVOR MERRIDEN

CAPSTONE

First published 2001 by
Capstone Publishing Limited (A Wiley Company)
8 Newtec Place
Magdalen Road
Oxford OX4 1RE
United Kingdom
http://www.capstoneideas.com

CIP catalogue records for this book are available from the British Library
and the US Library of Congress

ISBN 1-84112-104-5

Typeset in 11/15 pt New Baskerville by
Sparks Computer Solutions Ltd, Oxford, UK
http://www.sparks.co.uk
Printed and bound by
TJ International Ltd, Padstow, Cornwall

This book is printed on acid-free paper

To Melanie, for her love, patience and good humor
during the writing of this book

CONTENTS

ACKNOWLEDGMENTS

This is a book about Nokia, but not a book written with any official help from Nokia. It was decided early on that "official" help could risk a series of bland interviews with carefully briefed spokespeople. In the event, individual Nokia employees were helpful and open when approached about the company's methods of doing business. For those that helped, many thanks.

Basically, that this book was written at all is thanks to four people. Firstly there is Ken Langdon at KPL, who helped to prepare early drafts of many of the chapters. Ken simply bowled me over with his fanatical dedication and relentless enthusiasm in the face of trying circumstances and a very tight timetable. I look forward to working with you again.

Thanks also to Mark Allin and Richard Burton at Capstone. They had the idea in the first place for doing a book on Nokia and skillfully cajoled the project along at vital moments to a happy conclusion.

Last, but definitely not least, a big thanks to my wife, Melanie. She has put up with my regular vanishing act into the study at evenings and weekends. Thank you for your patience.

Trevor Merriden
Clapham, London

◆ OVERVIEW ◆

Do you want to make your organization more successful by learning from another company's spectacular success? Of course you do. And you could no better than look at Nokia, the world's leading supplier of mobile phones and a titan of European and world technology. In business for more than a hundred years, though not without one or two scares along the way, Nokia has developed a successful method of working that has fuelled its astonishing growth. And this in an industry that it only wholeheartedly committed itself to eight years ago.

CHOOSING THE RIGHT BUSINESS

66 F ocus" is possibly the most overused word in business jargon. It's so easy to talk about concentrating on core objectives, but very difficult to put all the good intentions into practice. And until the 1990s, Nokia was anything but focused.

The company's history goes back to the year 1865, with the establishment of a forest industry enterprise in the southwestern corner of Finland. Later, in 1898 and 1912 respectively, a rubber company and a cable manufacturer independently began their operations. Gradually the ownership of these three companies became concentrated into the hands of a few people. They were finally merged in 1967 to form the unwieldy conglomerate we know today as the Nokia Corporation. Even then, however, it became harder rather than easier to understand what sort of company Nokia was, as plastics production joined the Nokia family in the 1970s, followed later by a move into metal products and ventilation systems. Then in 1982, Nokia acquired Finnish Chemicals. Here, then, was a right old ragbag of businesses. It had something for everyone, but meant little to anyone.

The seeds of the Nokia we all know today were only sown in the 1980s, through yet more acquisitions which strengthened the conglomerate's position in the telecommunications and consumer electronics markets. In 1988 Nokia bought the data systems division of Ericsson, a move that suddenly made it the largest information technology company – in Scandinavia.

In 1990, Jorma Ollila, Nokia's current chairman, was put in charge of the mobile phones business. According to *Fortune* magazine[1] Ollila became convinced very quickly of its potential: "What I was told by my seniors was 'Look, you get six months to make a proposal on whether we sell it or what we do with this business.' After four months I said 'No we are not going to sell this one.'"

Ollila's passionate commitment to the potential of mobile technology soon began to make sense in a rather dramatic manner. In the early 1990s, with the conglomerate near bankruptcy from a deep global recession, the twin pillars propping up Nokia were the telecommunications and mobile phone departments. In 1992, Ollila was appointed chief executive officer and the changes began.

Ollila's passionate commitment to the potential of mobile technology soon began to make sense in a rather dramatic manner.

In his first year Ollila decided to have mobile phones and telecommunications as the core of the business. More importantly, he decided to divest it of all the non-core operations. The company was steering itself into "focus" – and how. If you look at the make up of the company in 1988 and compare it with 2000, you will see that the businesses of telecommunications and mobile phones has gone from ten percent of sales to the entire business.

NOKIA'S CHANGE IN FOCUS BETWEEN 1988 AND 2000

Business (1988)	Percentage of sales	Survived?	Business (2000)
Floorings	1%	No	Transmission systems
Chemicals	2%	No	Fixed networks
Machinery	4%	No	Access networks
Electrical wholesale	4%	No	Wireless/mobile data
Mobile telephones	5%	**Yes**	Tetra networks and terminals
Telecommunications	5%	**Yes**	GSM networks
Rubber	6%	No	Smart traffic products
Information systems	23%	No	Multimedia
Cables	9%	No	Internet
Paper	10%	No	Digital exchanges
Consumer electronics	31%	No	Mobile phones Base stations

RIDING THE UPWAVE – AND BEATING THE PANTS OFF THE OPPOSITION

Ollila's decision proved inspired. The phenomenal growth in demand for mobile technology meant that over the five years from 1995 to 1999, sales figures multiplied by three times, profits rose by nearly five times and the share price soared – at one point as much as 25 times. But unlike many companies in this high-growth sector, Nokia has being paying good dividends (more than a sixfold increase) instead of merely promising them for the future.

NOKIA'S DIVIDEND PAYMENTS

	Sales EURm	Profits EURm	Stock price EUR Helsinki exchanges at end of year	Dividends EURm
1995	6,191	830	7.14	151
1996	6,613	655	11.27	176
1997	8,849	1,408	16.31	378
1998	13,326	2,456	52.14	586
1999	19,772	3,845	180.00	931

The rapid growth of the mobile technology industry has surprised everyone in terms of the speed of mobile phones – even Nokia itself.

Nokia has said

"In 1992, we anticipated that not more than 50 million handsets would be sold world-wide in 1999. The actual figure was more than 250 million."[2]

Ilkka Pukkila, a director of Nokia Networks

Now the company's predictions are becoming bolder – more than a billion in 2002. The year 2000 saw the arrival of Wireless Application Protocols (WAP). This standard supports the growth of the mobile Internet, as handsets change from voice devices to voice/data combined, with an expected emphasis on use as a data device.

Nokia has said

"This year the number of WAP phones sold – around 30 million – will be higher than the number of laptops sold."[3]

Ilkka Pukkila, a director of Nokia Networks

Some might say that Nokia was in the right market at the right time. But healthy markets tend to attract healthy competitors and Nokia has beaten the pants off all of them. The value that the stock market puts on a company can often be over generous and sometimes harsh, but no one has yet come up with a better way of measuring what a company is worth. According to its stock market valuation since 1995, Nokia has enjoyed twice the growth in stock price of its Scandinavian rival Ericsson, and ten times that of the US giant Motorola. And just to rub it in, Nokia was named in 2000 as the world's leading technology company in a survey by the US magazine *BusinessWeek*.

CHANGING THE BUSINESS

Nokia has said

"Until now the winners in mobile communications have been European companies, the winners in consumer electronics have been Japanese and the winners in the Internet have been American. The question now is who will master the total scope best? That's the new game we are entering."[4]

Matti Alahuhta, president of Nokia mobile phones

Matti Alahuhta's quote could easily sum up why Nokia is so successful. It is a recognition of a continuous need to change Nokia to meet the challenge of new markets. This recognition shows itself in an impressive list of firsts. Their emphasis remains, as we will see, on excellence of design and innovation. Ollila's vision that mobile phones would become mass consumer products meant that Nokia needed to become a brand – consumers like and buy brands, especially new brands. The technology-driven company had to change into an innovative one, with a holistic approach to new products.

NOKIA FIRSTS[5]

1992   The Nokia 100 series, the first family of hand-portable phones for all analog networks

1992   The Nokia 1011, the first digital hand-portable phone for GSM networks

1994   The Nokia 2100 series, the first digital hand-portable phones supporting data, fax and the Short Message System

1996   The Nokia 9000 Communicator, the first all-in-one phone, fax, calendar, e-mail and Internet in hand-portable size.

1997   The Nokia 8110i, the first mobile phone with a dynamic menu supporting Smart Messaging

1997   The Nokia 3810, the first mobile phone specially designed for Asian consumers, with a full-graphics display and Asian language interfaces

1997   The Nokia Cellular Card Phone, a PC card with a built-in GSM phone. For voice and data communications in a notebook PC and in integrated solutions

1998   The Nokia 5100 series, the first mobile phone with user-changeable covers

1998   The Nokia 9110 Communicator, the first hand-held mobile terminal supporting wireless imaging

1999   The Nokia 7110, the first mobile phone compliant with the Wireless Application Protocol 1.1, which gives access to mobile Internet services

1999   The Nokia 8210, the first phone designed and launched in co-operation with the fashion industry

---

Now the next round of innovation is underway. To maintain its position on the world stage Nokia will have to cope with the next revolution, the third-generation equipment that brings the strands of mobile technology together.

Even if you think that Nokia got lucky being in a rapidly expanding market, there was no luck in the fact that the company decided to focus its efforts entirely in the direction of the mobile Internet. And there was no luck in the way in which it has consistently outperformed its rivals. Nokia has learnt lessons throughout its history. These lessons are outlined in the following chapters.

Comment on – *insights*

As I spoke to people in and out of Nokia I have had some insights about what we can learn. These are not necessarily attributable to one source, so I have called them comments.

NOTES

1   Nokia mobile phones, Nokia 2000.

2   Christopher Brown-Jones, *Financial Times*, July 2000.

3   See note 2.

4   See note 2.

5   See note 1.

One

COMBINE LEADERSHIP AND BRAVERY TO ACHIEVE PERFECT VISION

Understanding what those at Nokia mean by leadership is crucial to understanding what makes the company tick. Leadership at Nokia means far more than achieving dominance in the marketplace, or having a strong personality at the helm. People at Nokia want to lead and shape debate in every aspect of their work. They lead through setting down clear policies to achieve objectives and then having the bravery to pursue some radical initiatives. For those at Nokia, leadership plus bravery equals the corporate equivalent of 20/20 vision. And that's a pretty handy thing for any company to have.

Leadership is a word frequently used by those at Nokia. Of course Nokia wants market leadership but then, one might argue, what company doesn't? Yet there is something a little different about Nokia when it comes to leadership. To understand what that "something" is, is absolutely crucial to an understanding what makes Nokia tick.

Leadership at Nokia means leadership of a broad church of stakeholders. This involves their employees, as you might expect, but it also means leadership of shareholders, suppliers, employees, its community role and last, but definitely not least, the customer. To all intents and purposes this is, of course, the stakeholder model of working, much loved by organizations such as Tomorrow's Company (www.tomorrowscompany.com).

Critics say that the stakeholder model is just a list of high ideals and to a point that is true. The stakeholder model is not, by any stretch of the imagination, unique to Nokia and nobody at the company could seriously claim that it is. What those at Nokia do claim is that while other companies talk a good stakeholder game, Nokia is uniquely effective at putting it into practice.

To understand why this it is so we need a refresher on Nokia's history of leadership.

THE ROOTS OF BRAVE LEADERSHIP AT NOKIA

What does the 1980s mean to you? Ronald Reagan, Margaret Thatcher, the New Romantics, and the rise of the city slicker talking into mobile phones the size of a house brick. Fast forward to the 1990s and what of these has survived? Clinton and Blair, grunge and garage, dress-down Fridays and much smaller, neater mobile phones. It's early days in the new century for politicians and pop, but so far mobiles are smaller still, incorporate wireless application protocols (WAP) – which allow the phone user to access the Internet – and come in a variety of shapes and colors and ringing tones (some more annoying than others). The evolution of the mobile phone is startling. It is a good product, superbly tailored to meet the individual needs of customers. That this is so has much to do with the way Nokia has consistently kept one step ahead in understanding those needs.

That in turn has had much to do with brave leadership decisions taken at the start of the 1990s. Any old fool can make a lot of money with the right product and a wiser fool can make the good times last a little longer with a good business strategy. But only the truly wise can achieve success over a long period. This chapter shows that Nokia is more than just some lucky company riding the wave of a growing market, and definitely in the latter category.

Nokia's successes can be traced back to 1992, when newly appointed president and chief executive officer, Jorma Ollila, decided to transform the company radically. Many chief executives in the 1990s have tried to do the same thing, with varying degrees of success. "Focus" became a byword for corporate strategy across the world, as chief executives sought to concentrate on their core operations and cut out anything that didn't seem to fit the core.

Ollila had the same idea – he wanted to focus too – but with one crucial difference. Ollila wanted Nokia to focus on something that at the time was a *non-core operation*. Nokia, he decided, should devote its entire operations to telecommunications. That was a radical step – back in 1986 only 15 percent of Nokia's activities were channeled towards telecommunications and by the early 1990s it remained an unwieldy conglomerate of rubber products and wireless technologies.

Why was Ollila so bold? Part of the answer lay in his own instincts and part of it was based on the words of his mentor. Ollila's business strategy is founded on that of Kari Kairamo, the man who recruited him to Nokia in 1984. Kairamo was the managing director of Nokia. Kairamo wanted to turn Nokia into an electronics firm. But Kairamo never lived to enact his vision. He committed suicide in 1988 and Ollila took up his cause.

Even so, Ollila didn't take over the helm of Nokia until 1992 and when he did the outlook was unpromising. The company had been teetering on the edge of bankruptcy and the domestic economy was in depression, largely because the Soviet Union, Finland's giant neighbor, was disintegrating into economic chaos. This was a moment when leadership of any company in Finland involved no little bravery. And although the results of Ollila's efforts are there for all to see today, it was by no means obvious ten years earlier that Nokia should be any more a "focused" electronics firm than a "focused" rubber company. And in the teeth of a savage recession, others suggested that

KEY NOKIA FACTS

Nokia comprises three business groups Nokia Networks, Nokia Mobile phones, and Nokia Communications Products. In addition they also have a separate Nokia Ventures Organisation and the corporate research unit, Nokia Research Centre.

Nokia Networks develops and manufactures a range of infrastructure solutions for a variety of customers including fixed operators, mobile operators and Internet service providers. They also supply network management solutions and systems integration.

Nokia Mobile Phones is the world's largest mobile phone manufacturer with nine factories spread across three continents and sales in over 130 countries.

Nokia Communications Products has two units: Nokia Multimedia Terminals, making digital terminals for interactive multimedia applications and digital broadcasting, and Nokia Display Products offering advanced PC and workstation monitors.

Nokia Ventures Organisation works with partners to explore new business areas and invest in, amongst others, start up businesses that are beyond the scope of Nokia's three business units.

Nokia Research Centre interacts with all Nokia business units to explore new technologies and product/system concepts. They also work on how to exploit these in actual product development undertaken in the business units.

In 1999 67 percent of their nearly 20 billion Euro sales came from Phones with Nokia Networks at 29 percent and with the other 4 percent coming from the rest.

Nokia should focus on neither but should instead protect itself by diversifying further.

Comment on – *vision*

Peter Drucker has said that any successful company has at some point been led by someone who made a brave decision. He could have added that continued success depends on reviewing that brave decision – and having the courage to alter the vision again before things go wrong.

Ollila and his team stuck to their guns. Firstly, they saw the opportunities in the liberalization of the telecommunications market in the way that few other companies did at the time. They had the bravery to pioneer the development of the Global System for Mobiles (GSM) network as a standard means of communications across borders. By the early 1990s Nokia suddenly had a great product at exactly the right moment in their history. That they had arrived at that point was no accident. For some time Nokia had been investing heavily in research and development into the GSM. Now, to make sure that they had the potential to exploit their opportunity, Ollila made the far-sighted decision to invest heavily in innovation and design of the product. This meant that the product had the potential for marketing across the globe.

On taking over, Ollila sold off other parts of the business and concentrated solely on mobile technologies. The way in which he did this, however, shows that a black-and-white approach to what is to stay and go at a company has no place in Nokia strategy. Ollila recognized that the businesses Nokia had been in but was about to sell had been successful at some point over many years. Again this was no accident. So before he sold anything off, he sent his new management team to examine what they could learn from the longevity and experience of the businesses. He wanted to make sure that he was not throwing out any valuable management process or lesson that could be applied within the new Nokia. This led to the discovery and documentation of the Nokia Way, of which more later.

WHAT BRAVERY REALLY MEANS

What does a golfer do if he or she loses confidence in a particular club? Frequently, a few bad strikes with the driver will lead players into fearing or even expecting failure. This fear of failure sometimes makes the chance of failure more likely. At that point your average golfer abandons the club. Extend this principle through the whole set of clubs, and eventually the only club you will use is your putter – you cannot fluff that club and no one will expect you to hit very far. Any organization that, either accidentally or on purpose, develops a culture of fear and blame, runs the risk of having the staff only using their putters.

Nokia's philosophy on bravery is based around the eradication of ... fear of failure.

Nokia's philosophy on bravery is based around the eradication of this sort of fear of failure. Evidence for this is found at the Nokia's research and development centers. The company fully recognizes that innovation and leadership means going into research areas that, eventually, turn out to be dead ends with many projects started and finished with no tangible contribution to the company's bottom line. What happens to the project manager when the experiment is

MORE ABOUT JORMA

Jorma Ollila is 50 years old. He is the chairman of the board and chief executive officer, and chairman of the group executive board. He held the president and chief executive officer posts until 1999. He studied at the University of Helsinki and gained his first taste of leadership during this period when he became chairman of the Finnish Students union in the mid-1970s. After a seven-year stint at Citibank he rose rapidly to the top of Nokia. Ollila is considered a hero in Finland; he sits on the board of five companies, and has been on the board of a number of others. He also has assisted with the management of many industrial associations and other public Finnish bodies such as his chairmanship of the Helsinki University of Technology. He has had official honors bestowed on him by the governments of five different countries. He is a man of simple tastes who lives in a modest house just outside Helsinki. His summer cottage is equipped with an outside toilet that he constructed himself.

abandoned? Nothing. Except encouragement to try another route. No one gets shot.

Comment on – *blame*

Getting rid of a blame culture is easier said than done. If you listen to how people talk about their business and their colleagues, you can easily recognize the underlying fear and the search for the scapegoat. Creating a blame-free attitude may mean taking things almost to the point of political correctness. A blame-free culture usually avoids threatening words and prefers always to be forward looking in its use of language. It is also partly a reliance on the appraisal system that ensures that people are in the right jobs with the right skills and training.

Such a blame-free culture keeps people trying everything. For example, Nokia brought out the Communicator – an innovative product but one without high-volume sales potential at the time of its development. It was one of the many Nokia firsts, an all-in-one phone, fax, calendar, and Internet in hand-portable size. Nokia spent the money and went through a lot of pain for little return in the first instance. In the end they found themselves at the forefront of the product market of digital convergence. When asked if Nokia was losing its entrepreneur spirit, Pekka Ala Pietila, Nokia president, used the Communicator as an example of a product that had much invested in it heavily. "I can hardly contemplate what we have spent on the Communicator," he said.

Others have said

" A young person should know the limit of his or her authority, when to exceed it, and to make sure that he or she is right."

The chairman of a FTSE 100 company

Bravery with the Communicator is tied in with the freedom to act. The product manager on the Communicator never actually had approval to develop it, according to Lindsay Brook, human resources manager in the UK. He did not need it. Nokia people are encouraged to have a go. This means that a lot of projects get so far down the road. If they do get stopped, there is no management witch-hunt and no one gets blamed.

Communicating a "blame free" strategy through the organization produces a blame free culture and translates bravery down through the organization. A Nokia product manager started a high level of research and development and kept going down a particular road for some two years. He had spent a lot of resources on the project when he realized that the project did not fit with the emerging corporate strategy. Whereas in many other companies he would have gone ahead with his baby, in Nokia, protected by its respect for the individual value, he cancelled the project and told the board it had become non-strategic.

In another example, a manager developing a product for the US market had to go to the Nokia board to discuss the development of a particular project. He was not satisfied with some quality issues and actually recommended to the board that they not approve the development of the product until the quality issues had been resolved. This delayed the product but was strategically the right thing to do. There are plenty of other organizations where the project manager would have kept the board in the dark, given that most managers would have moved on before the quality problems became apparent.

This bravery – call it straight talking without fear of reprisal – at all levels, helps Nokia managers get the right balance between long-term and short-term thinking, which benefits everyone in the organization.

WHAT LEADERSHIP REALLY MEANS

Bravery in leadership is one thing, but what about leadership style? The Nokia leadership style is characterized by its flexibility. Everyone recognizes that there is the time for a strong lead and a time for consensus building. If there is a revolution in one of the countries where your product plant is based, or a fire at a warehouse, it is not the time to call a focus group and find consensus. Equally, if you want to take bright engineers with you in terms of your strategy development, the way not to do it is to arrive at a planning meeting knowing that the only acceptable plan is inside the head of the senior person present. That's a waste of time for everyone.

The balance is to get things done by taking a dictatorial approach when necessary but wherever possible seeking opinions and consulting – particularly when the key to success is motivating people to buy into a strategy to achieve a vision. It is Nokia practice to announce a strategy change to a group of individuals and then for that group immediately to consult with the next level down on the implications of the change for them. What this means is that everyone recognizes their involvement in how the company is managed while recognizing that in the end decisions have to be made sometimes very fast owing to the nature of the business.

It is Nokia practice to announce a strategy change to a group of individuals and then for that group immediately to consult with the next level down on the implications of the change for them.

Phil Brown, head of Nokia Mobile Phones' UK marketing and sales division talks about the speed with which strategy is passed down the management structure. This is essential because on a broad subject like the global information society, different parts of Nokia have to develop their own versions of the strategy. There are checks and balances, such as the company scorecard mechanism, which are designed to see whether the overall objectives of the company are being translated into specific goals further down the company. But the important thing in terms of leadership style is that managers are allowed to deliver the message in their own way. The manager must achieve results, but he is considered in the first instance to be best placed to deliver the message so as to achieve these results.

HOW LEADERSHIP AND BRAVERY EQUALS VISION

Example 1: Nokia and the Euro

When Finland's government pledged in 1995 to secure a place among the founders of the European single currency, ministers knew they could count on unswerving support from Nokia. Several Finnish companies, notably the large pulp and paper producers, were initially cool towards the Euro, as some are now. But the leadership at Nokia never hid its enthusiasm for the single currency, seeing a great opportunity from fewer currencies in what was developing into a global market, geared up for the transition from markka to Euros for more than four years until its formal introduction in 1999.

Nokia regarded the Euro as a commercial advantage, believing the cost of adjusting to the single currency is vastly outweighed by the prospective financial benefits. It had good reason to see things this way. Of its seven largest markets, four – Germany, Italy, France and Finland – are inside the Euro club. The company derives more than half its annual sales from Europe.

Nokia's effort began in earnest in 1996 with the creation of an internal task force, a well-used management technique in the company, to analyze the implications of switching to Euros. At an early stage the Nokia leadership decided to pursue a swift Big Bang-type conversion to the new currency. The reasoning was that a staggered switch within the company during the transitional period between the currency's formal arrival and the arrival of Euro notes and coins in Euro zone high streets to be potentially risky.

The leadership strategy therefore meant having the bravery to do far more than the minimum necessary. Leadership internally was, of course, a major focus. In attempting to take their people with them, it issued a company booklet explaining the purpose and practical implications of the new currency. Training courses started early in 1998, targeted primarily at staff in finance, legal and cash management functions. The biggest challenge was the adoption of a new group-accounting computer system, one capable of handling Euros. Until 1999 Nokia operated different accounting systems in various countries. However, the advent of the Euro persuaded it to adopt a single, worldwide system also capable of recognizing the new currency. Even with salaries, although paid in national currencies until the end of the changeover period, it includes Euros alongside the domestic currency on salary slips.

Nokia also took the initiative with its customers, suppliers and sub-contractors. It urged them to convert to Euro invoicing as soon as possible after 1999. They did not, however, coerce their business partners to switch. They didn't really need to. Given their power and size, some would argue, it is little surprise that in most cases they have been successful.

Example 2: Help underdeveloped countries and help yourselves

Global market leadership depends on getting huge sales of popular products into the developed world. It also means gaining acceptance that your product is important elsewhere. The best companies not only make their products relevant to consumers in the less developed countries, but go out of their way to demonstrate their commitment to the country to which it is selling. Nokia did this so well that in 1997 International Media Partners and ING Barings presented it with a special award.

The award was presented to Jorma Ollila as the chief executive of a company "with headquarters in the developed world whose expansion into emerging markets has best shown how these markets can contribute to corporate revenues and profitability and also benefit the countries involved."

Others have said

"Successful businesses today recognise both the potential value emerging markets can play in the growth of a company and the role they play within the dynamics of a world economy. Nokia has capitalised on the merging of technology and service to expand into these new markets and sets an excellent example for competitive multinational corporations."

Jacques Kemp, chairman of the Regional Management Committee for ING Barings in Europe, the Middle East and Africa

Combined with fixed telecommunications where feasible, digital and cellular phone technology is arguably providing countries lacking a developed infrastructure with effective and modern telecommunication. There is certainly a demand for this infrastructure. Much of Nokia's growth can be attributed to its strength and presence in the world's fastest-growing economies. In capturing the lead in these markets, Nokia has led the competition with innovative technologies such as the introduction of the first Asian language interface in mobile phones and the erection of production facilities in, for example, Brazil, Hungary and China.

One other leadership accolade to cement the picture: Nokia has been named as one of the 100 best companies in the world by *Industry Week*'s Global Leadership Forum in 1998. It gained this because of "its overall position in the mobile phone market, its dedication to research and development and its efforts to streamline operations to focus more and more on its global telecommunications business."

Example 3: Look after the planet, it's the only one we've got

Nokia's work in emerging countries forms part of a strong environmental policy. Nokia overseas factories aspire to the same standards as the stringent tests of ISO 9000 and others – whatever the requirements of the local country.

Nokia has said

"A commitment to environmental issues is integral to Nokia's corporate culture. It is our goal to develop advanced digital technology, products and services that have no undue environmental impact, are efficient in their consumption of energy and natural resources, or even help to conserve them."

No Limits, Nokia 1999 annual report.

We have read many such statements in other annual reports. (It's a bit like the cliché "our people are our greatest asset," which regularly appears in annual reports that, on another page, report the massive cost reductions achieved as a result of downsizing these great assets.)

Why you tend to believe Nokia is the investment of time and money in implementing the policy. Well, you can talk to their people most of whom, if it is relevant, have environmental issues somewhere in their objectives. Importantly you can also talk to their suppliers all of whom have visits and advice from Nokia experts helping them to make sure that raw materials and sub-assemblies conform with the Nokia strategy.

Finally you can look at environmental leadership in the simple logic of the policy itself. The focus of Nokia's environmental work is around all aspects of product life cycles. They look at the environmental consequences of the supply chain, the manufacturing process, packaging and end-of-life activities such as recycling. They have a program – the Design for Environment (DFE) program – whose goal is to minimize the use of energy and materials and maximize reuse and recycling.

Having said all that, any environmental objectives they mention are constrained by a reminder that all this has to be done without increasing cost or decreasing performance or quality.

ASK YOURSELF

Here are the key leadership points that Nokia tends to get right. How well does your organization do?

1 Real freedom from the blame culture.
2 Policies in place to achieve a balance of interests among all its stakeholders.
3 Involvement of everyone in agreeing the plan to achieve objectives.
4 Gaining a reputation for fair dealing in overseas markets.
5 Making sure that strategy is communicated down the organization in time.
6 Varying its leadership styles to match the situation.
7 Balancing its financial and other goals with building a reputation for being environmentally friendly.

Two

BATTLE HARD TO WIN THE CUSTOMER

Nokia succeeds in meeting the needs of its customers – and anticipating their future needs. It does this by thinking about their lifestyles. This chapter shows how this is done.

M any companies still do not formally manage their relationship with their customer.[1] Nokia does because it has to – and because it wants to. The following viewpoint from Nokia chairman Jorma Ollila, about how Nokia customers think, illustrates this.

Nokia has said

"It is all about making technology work ... to create benefits which we all crave. At the end of the day people don't care about the technology. They want their lives to be richer, more pleasurable and more effective. We are the ones who want to make all this happen."[2]

Jorma Ollila, Nokia chairman

Nokia's ability to focus on the bottom-line needs of the customer is crucial to its overall successes. Customer retention and satisfaction should both be increasingly crucial parts of any business. In so doing it expands its ability to breed customer loyalty to the Nokia brand. At the same time it provides them with a vital means of information to target their sales and marketing efforts.

IT'S ALL ABOUT LIFESTYLE ...

The first thing to think about is the staggering headline number of consumers. Both Nokia and Ericsson forecast that the number of global mobile phone subscribers will increase from the current 300 million to a billion by 2003.

This is where the number crunching stops when it comes to customers. There are as many different needs as there are customers. Breaking the numbers down is not the whole answer either. Nigel Litchfield, senior vice-president of Nokia Mobile Phone in Asia Pacific says that sometimes segmentation of the market into different types of customers and then producing the products you think they want is not enough by itself.

Both Nokia and Ericsson forecast that the number of global mobile phone subscribers will increase from the current 300 million to a billion by 2003.

Today lifestyles are the broad backcloth against which purchasing decisions are made. And lifestyles are changing rapidly. It is no longer enough to divide markets by gender, age and income because it says nothing about consumer needs. This is encapsulated in what Litchfield says below.

Nokia has said

"People at Nokia need to understand how customers live their lives, what are their attitudes their lifestyle, behaviour and beliefs … it is the individual value systems, that we are seeking to understand."

Nigel Litchfield, senior vice-president of Nokia Mobile Phone in Asia Pacific[3]

Lifestyle consideration have become so important to the Nokia Way of thinking about the customer, because it helps to pinpoint coming changes in the psychology of a purchasing decision or a feeling of satisfaction for the customer. Thinking lifestyle effectively means that the company is able to pinpoint psychological changes in consumer attitudes toward its products. "The most important thing," says Litchfield, "is to understand the key drivers of the customer, such as what motivates them and excites them."

According to Litchfield, Nokia has been at the forefront of this somewhat esoteric approach. For some years, he says, Nokia has been bold enough to ask some pretty basic questions repeatedly. These questions are those such as "why do you communicate?", "what are the benefits of you mobile phone", and "whom do you communicate with on your mobile phone?" The questions are asked in order to scrutinize consumer behavior and needs.

Comment on – *basic questions*

Asking the most basic of questions, about why consumers do what they do, may seem like an obvious course of action. Yet many companies fail to even consider the psychology behind complex purchasing decisions. This is particularly true in the field of new technology, where the reasons behind a purchase may not be obvious. For example, many young people use their mobile phones for text messaging rather than phone calls, yet the extent of this trend was something which many in the mobile phone industry were initially slow to understand.

The rise in the number of users by 700 million in a little over three years will be driven by a huge rise in the number of young style-conscious users. As one beleaguered Finnish parent says of mobile phone-wielding youngsters:

Others have said

"Today the prerequisite for being cool is to have a mobile phone. It is totally uncool not to have one or to have the wrong brand."[4]

These youngsters may have a cool phone but they don't use them all the time to make calls. Half of young users' mobile phone bills are accounted for by sending text messages rather than actually speaking.

"Today the prerequisite for being cool is to have a mobile phone. It is totally uncool not to have one or to have the wrong brand."

Of course young customers are not homogeneous in their wants. For example the high-flying student may want a phone that opens into a palmtop computer capable of sending e-mail and faxes, while the poser may want the Nokia 8110, with its tiny handset and sleek, silver-colored case. Similarly the needs of the young consumer are again completely different from those wants of the business user.

Dominic Strowbridge is a director at one of Nokia's major rivals Motorola. Like those at Nokia, Strowbridge is keen on the lifestyle imperative when selling to the consumer. He thinks that there are four main types of lifestyle to consider. We have:

◆ the techno-enthusiast, who can't wait to get his or her hands on the latest gizmos;

◆ the time and information manager, the busy professional who wants to run her life more efficiently;

◆ the personal connector, who just wants to stay in touch with friends and family at all times; and

◆ the status or style seeker, better known to the rest of us as posers.

Others have said

"From this, those in the mobile technology business can get to the heart of what the end-users want. The techie may want the personal digital assistant, the time and information guy may want unified messaging. And whatever they want now, there's only going to be more rather than less variety in what the consumer will want in the future."[5]

Dominic Strowbridge director at Motorola

... SO LET'S GET PERSONAL

Strowbridge's observation is a good one. What one means by "the market" is no longer clear when it comes to mobile technologies and there will be more variety, not less, in the future. An examination of customer attitudes, says Litchfield, notes not only that the days when mobile phone makers could offer only one mobile phone that served everybody's needs are over. This is a market in which there are no killer applications that serve all. Everybody is different. Everybody wants their own personal needs satisfied when making their purchasing decision. The key to success in achieving customer satisfaction lies in the way that Nokia identifies the different forms of lifestyle – and then meets the needs of each.

> The key to success in achieving customer satisfaction lies in the way that Nokia identifies the different forms of lifestyle – and then meets the needs of each.

Because of its respect for the lifestyle criterion, Nokia believes strongly in personalization for people's needs. All companies, Nokia included, need to build long-term relationships with their existing customers, and also to target new ones, and to do this they have to deal with customer needs and wants on an individual level. For example the increased options for personalizing phones, perhaps with color or ring tone, has increasingly become a well-known feature of Nokia products. Frank Nuovo is the chief designer at Nokia Mobile Phones. He gets excited when it comes to looking at the opportunities for design created by new technologies. But he adds that the Nokia system makes it unlikely that he will be getting carried away.

Nokia has said

"While technologies are advancing rapidly [they] have no value in themselves. They only attain value in the context of fulfilling human needs. People must gain real benefits from them. That is what our challenge is all about: understanding peoples' needs and using our technology competencies to come up with applications that make their lives better … In the near future this trend towards more numerous personalisation possibilities will multiply … That's why we are continually deepening our understanding of the consumer."[6]

Frank Nuovo, chief designer at Nokia Mobile Phones

CUSTOMERS ARE RUTHLESS …

It is not just the corporate world that is ruthless these days. The customer is even more so. Rule number one for customer satisfaction for Nokia is that you have never won. Why is this? Because the number of customers is increasing so rapidly that its needs are changing and, as we have seen above, becoming more sophisticated. The customer increasingly expects his or her complex wants to be satisfied in full – or else.

Customers know that there are many different touch points for contact and interaction in finding out about the range of products on offer. This means that there have never been so many threats to any company's relationship with it customer, Nokia included. Customers will make their decisions through a combination of the rational and the emotional. They can change their brand easily for superior practical benefits, and will not hesitate to do so. A recent survey showed that most companies see the heightened consumer demand for value as the number one market challenge in the year 2000.[7]

Close behind the consumer demand for value in the survey is the challenge of overcoming erosion of customer loyalty to the brand. However, if there is little to choose between product then product loyalty plays a part. Loyalty for Nokia is built through good customer service – working hard on the relationship with the customer. To do so, it has to be dedicated. Ruthless indeed.

... SO NOKIA MUST BE RUTHLESS TOO

Nokia keeps on asking the questions because it assumes nothing in the decision-making behavior of the customer. The number of customers is growing, their lifestyle needs are forever changing and the nature of their demands are becoming more sophisticated.

Obviously it pays to know your customers and keep them happy. New markets are evolving as lifestyles change and the trick is always to try to understand the identity of the next market segment to venture into. Fortunately, one of Nokia's chief selling points is that customers know that when it comes to Nokia, they will get the latest thinking first on a product. Pekka Ala-Pietila, Nokia president, says that the company has maximized the value for the customer through investing heavily in spending on R&D. At Nokia, R&D accounts for around ten percent of turnover, much of which has added new customer benefits.

Nokia has said

"People appreciate new functions and it is important to be first with them, especially as 40 per cent of sales today are replacement sales; in 1990 it was four per cent."

Frank Nuovo, chief designer at Nokia Mobile Phones

This often means some ruthless decision making along the way about which products to keep and which to dispense with. To Ala-Pietila and Nokia, customer satisfaction essentially means abandoning traditional product cycles and continually updating and refreshing its portfolio. That way, he says, Nokia can prevent handsets becoming just any old commodity and can create more of a feeling of genuine innovation.

It is also important to realize that because of the growing cult of the consumer as an individual, there will never be an "application" that will keep everybody happy. The best that any Nokia product can do is to provide a maximum combination of options.

Nokia has said

"Don't waste your time looking for killer applications. They don't exist today. There are no global or even local killer applications, but what we can do is provide a killer cocktail of many applications to give the consumer the most choice possible within a single product"

Niklas Savander, vice-president, Mobile Internet Applications,

Nokia Networks

The benefit of winning customer loyalty through the use of such cocktails is there for all to see. According to CSC,[8] a five percent increase in customer retention can boost profits by 60 percent in just five years. Moreover the cost of acquiring new customers is five to ten times that of retaining your best customers.

GETTING A LITTLE EXTRA HELP

Consumers are confident and happy and are spending like they haven't in years. And the vast amount of available information about them from all this spending, allied with new technology that captures their purchasing decisions, has given retailers the ability to understand and predict consumer behaviors in powerful new ways. It has allowed alert companies to reach into the private spaces of consumers. For Nokia, the effective use of such information has resulted in the posting of some very impressive sales figures among retailers of all types. It takes the right information in the right hands at the right time to build a strong community of customer relationships, reduce the cost of sale, and capture market share. Unprecedented customer knowledge fuels targeted and more effective marketing programs and better customer service. The latest customer relationship management

Nokia has never been shy of getting in outside expertise in any area of its business, and customer relationship management is no different.

(CRM) techniques help make this possible. But where to get them from?

No company has the monopoly on wisdom when it comes to using this information. Nokia has never been shy of getting in outside expertise in any area of its business, and customer relationship management is no different. Hence it was no surprise with the company teamed up with ICL in February 2000. The two companies have formed a new company, which is two-thirds owned by ICL and one-third by Nokia. The joint venture is aimed, among other things, at developing systems and service for its customer relationship management needs.

ICL is a London-based wholly-owned subsidiary of Fujitsu. It is a global IT services company which designs, builds and operates information systems and service for customers in the retail, finance, government telecoms, utilities and travel markets. The company has operations in over 40 countries and employs over 22,000 people. The combined company implements customer solutions that engage technology in all aspects of the business today, by helping Nokia improve relationships with not only the end-user customers, but also with their clients, business partners and staff. The agreement marked a significant expansion in the existing co-operation between two companies that are already very close. Tarmo Ruosteenoja, vice-president of Nokia Information Management, says: "The mission of Nice-business Solutions Finland Oy was to implement e-Business and customer relationship management solutions and services that support Nokia's strategy. Nokia chose ICL as its partner because of the company's impressive track record in the e-Business area."

ASK YOURSELF

Here are some things that Nokia are very good at when it comes to tracking their new customers. Ask yourself these basic questions about the way you operate:

1 Do you know why your customers use your product, as well as who they are?

2 Do you know what they buy?

3 Do you know when they buy it?

4 Do you know what they don't buy – and why?

5 Do you know anything about how your customers live their lives?

6 Are you providing your employees with the right tools to capture and analyze critical customer data?

7 Do you take into account the views of your customers when developing your company's products?

8 Has the Internet made an impact on the way you handle your customers?

NOTES

1 ICL study as part of its annual *Captains of Industry Survey,* 9 March 2000.

2 P7, Nokia Annual Report 1999.

3 Nigel Litchfield was speaking at a Nokia press seminar and the CommunicAsia 99 in Singapore in July 1999.

4   "The Nordic Connection: how Nokia and Ericsson have rung rings around the world." From the *Independent,* 16 June 1999.

5   Dominic Strowbridge was speaking at the FT Mobile Technology summit in September 2000.

6   Nokia Annual Report 1999, p. 19.

7   *Retailing in e-time,* the tenth annual retail technology study, 2000, p. 8.

8   From the Computer Sciences Corporation Web site, www.csc.com.

---◆---

Three

RESPECT THE INDIVIDUAL

---◆---

People at the top of Nokia say that their secret is the way in which they enable their people to work. Many companies say that they value the people who work for them, but few have such a well-documented statement of their people strategy. This is known as the Nokia Way.

Nokia has said

In trying to answer the question "what is Nokia's secret?" Nokia's chairman Jorma Ollila is almost mystical in his reply. "It's the way the organisation creates a meeting of minds among people. How do you send a message that this is a meritocracy, and this is a place where you are allowed to have a bit of fun, to think unlike the norm, where you are allowed to make a mistake? First of all it comes from how the management team works, how they communicate. Is it a political set up, one with lots of hidden agendas? I think we have had through the years, particularly through the 1990s, a strong culture of 'none of that nonsense.'"[1]

AS FLAT AS A PANCAKE

Look at the way more traditional companies than Nokia organize themselves in terms of their people. They put command and control at the heart of the policy and, generally speaking, few managers concern themselves with employee involvement and participation.

Nowadays of course, the trend in most companies is towards less hierarchical structures, striving to put the emphasis on getting the most out of the talents and skills of people. Flatter structures encourage much higher involvement with the running of the business and stress a customer and business-oriented approach at all levels and functions. Nokia's hierarchical structure, considering its size, is as flat as a pancake.

Nokia has said

"We have a very flat organisation. My boss's boss's boss is Jorma Ollila. He can go and pick up our scorecard from the intranet whenever he wants – and so can anyone else."

Phil Brown, head of Nokia Mobile Phones' UK marketing and sales

This flat structure is a pre-condition to the effective operation of the way in which Nokia treats its staff. This is known as the Nokia Way of working. The Nokia Way essentially comprises three elements:

◆ processes aimed at operational efficiency;

◆ competencies; and

◆ Nokia Values.

Strategy drives the operations, or processes, of the company and is then fine-tuned by the feedback senior management get from these operations. But supporting this are the Nokia Values and competencies.

Processes

A flat, networked organization allows the company to maintain speed and flexibility in decision making.

Nokia has said

"We go to these conferences and talk for a day about a certain issue, for example, the way in which the global information society is affecting our business. But – and here's the point – we then sit down the next day and work out in smaller groups precisely what the previous day meant for the strategy of selling mobile phones in Europe and Africa."

Phil Brown, head of Nokia Mobile Phones' UK marketing and sales

The managers attending the second day to which Brown refers then go away and translate a particular issue to fit those working in their own area. This is essential because, on a broad subject like the global information society, Nokia Networks will thinking about focusing attention on new systems protocols – for Nokia Ventures it could mean the purchase of certain companies and for Nokia Mobiles it will mean something else altogether.

Nowadays of course, the trend in most companies is towards less hierarchical structures, striving to put the emphasis on getting the most out of the talents and skills of people.

Managers are allowed to deliver the message in their own way – with the necessary speed and flexibility. How each message is delivered may be up to the individual, but delivered it must be. There are checks and balances within the Nokia system designed to see whether the overall objectives of the company are being translated into specific goals further down the company. They turn their innovations into specific actions. This global strategy is executed quickly and effectively.

Comment on – *recruitment*

It is very helpful to the recruitment process to have a summary of the attributes of the type of person the company wants. This makes certain that managers are not simply preferring their "type of person" which often really means appointing people similar to themselves. It is worth remembering that the recruitment of the wrong person can be up with the most expensive mistakes that a manager can make.

Now look at the personal qualities they look for in managers to enable this process to be successful – speed, quality, openness, integrity, teamwork, humility, accountability, responsibility and empowerment. These attributes, Nokia claim, ensure not only that the operation works effectively, but that it delivers the high-quality Nokia products and services that translate into customer satisfaction. This, in another good Nokia phrase gives them "value based leadership."[2]

In Nokia they prefer to think of decision making as a process, not a refuge of leadership.

In Nokia, we find management systems based on strong process thinking. They look for processes everywhere. They want to use the same process management principles and terminology throughout the company in order to make learning as efficient as possible.

Suppose someone somewhere in the company makes a difficult decision. In most companies, how they came to the decision would remain in the head of the decision maker, and he or she would have gone about the decision-making process in their own style. In Nokia they prefer to think of decision making as a process, not a refuge of leadership. The person goes through the process and records their thinking electronically. That decision then becomes part of the company's learning exercise.

Comment on – *sharing insights*

Sharing insights tests the attitude of a business, as well as its processes. Not only do you have to supply the means by which managers can teach others what they have learnt. You also have to persuade them that it does not threaten their unique contribution to the organization. You cannot share insights without running your company in an open management style.

Now make the information that the person gathered to make the decision (and the process that they went through to come to their conclusion) accessible to others. This should cut the time it takes for someone to make a similar decision. And, if the original decision maker moves to another organization, the information stays in the company rather than moving on with them.

This may sound like a bureaucratic nightmare but in fact constitutes a huge fund of collective corporate wisdom. Think about what Nokia has to get right to take this more enlightened approach. They need job designs that encourage work teams and job enrichment. They use parallel structures such as task forces to handle major business issues. They need flexibility and an open mind from everyone within the company – all part of the Nokia Way.

Competencies

Nokia maintains that every member of staff possesses certain skills that allow them to contribute to the company's aims. These skills are what enable them to succeed in their tasks. So, describe the ideal competencies to undertake the job, set the objectives of the individual and identify the gaps between the ideal and the person. You are then in a position to put training and development activities into place that close these gaps and create the required competencies – right? Not right according to Nokia. That prepares them for the job they are doing today in the environment that pertains today. Nokia concentrates on

KEY FACTS

In 1999 Nokia had on average 51,177 people (41,091 in 1998). Employees productivity ratios are as follows:

◆ sales per employee: 381,920 Euros (324,305 Euros); and
◆ profit per employee: 50,355 Euros (42,588 Euros).

Corresponding figures for arch rival Ericsson are:

◆ sales per employee: 239,756 Euros (212,332); and
◆ profit per employee: 18,802 Euros (21,915 Euros).

The average age of a Nokia employee is thirty-two.

the competencies it will require in the future as much as the ones they need right now.

Values

Nokia has said

"Our success is dependent on the fact that we trust each other. At Nokia, you won't be let down when you ask for help from your colleagues. Team effort helps us exceed customer expectations."

Inandik Kursat from Nokia Networks, Finland[2]

In 1992 when the process of concentrating on the hitherto non-core business of telecommunications was born, Ollila sold off all the other businesses which, in their own way, had been very successful. Ollila was concerned not to lose the virtues that had ensured the success of these businesses and determined to learn from them prior to letting them go. A senior team of people examined the businesses and agreed the four main values that had made them great. Thus, the Nokia values are not constructed by a guru in a this-will-be-the-new-tradition-starting-from-now way, but were genuinely discovered by looking at how the businesses had worked. These values, if observed, provide a self-perpetuating system for achieving and maintaining success.

> **The Nokia Way is to go the extra mile in terms of customer satisfaction.**

Central to the values discovered is:

◆ *Respect for the individual.* Nokia uses attention to this value as its way of getting rid of the corporate politics that allow managers to work hard towards objectives that suit them, but not the company as a whole. In other words it avoids witch-hunts and the blame culture. Part of this value is protected by careful attention to the values of people being interviewed for jobs in the company.

Nokia has said

"Nokia's strengths lie in our belief in the importance of the individual whether he or she is an employee, business partner or customer. Everyone is an individual, working together as a team."

Nokia Way, Values in action

Apart from respect for the individual, the other values are:

◆ *Customer satisfaction.* Nokia's philosophy on customers is simply stated. "Customers are the most important people at Nokia. They are not dependent on Nokia, but Nokia is dependent on them. Without its customers Nokia would not exist."[2] The Nokia Way is to go the extra mile in terms of customer satisfaction. For example, a sales manager is delivering the first shipment of products to a new supplier like a large phone warehouse. He decides to be there when the shipment arrives and arranges to meet his main contact there. The customer feels that Nokia regards this first deal as significant and he welcomes this additional attention. This customer satisfaction covers internal customers as well as external ones.

Comment on – *internal customers*

One problem that some companies fail to achieve is to make their people take internal customers as seriously as they take their paying ones. For as long as this is the case, an organization will fail to deliver efficient business processes. This means, amongst other things, having a complaints and feedback system that caters for internal as well as external customers.

◆ *Achievement*. What focuses the attention of Nokia people is striving to achieve. To do this they must understand the company's strategies and goals. They all work to specific and measurable objectives, and the value states "Nokia personnel have the right to know exactly what is expected of them."[2] This in turn leads to the realization of responsibility and accountability.

Comment on – *performance measures*

Even when a measure is difficult to quantify, you have to keep looking. Unless you can agree in advance how success will be precisely measured, you cannot achieve real accountability throughout the organization.

And everyone knows how he or she is doing, and how everyone else is doing for that matter. There is a company scoreboard mechanism, in which a number of key performance indicators – such as financial, personnel/organization, brand – are all set as targets at the local level. Management teams review these targets every month, and more importantly they sit on the company's intranet and everyone has access to them.

Nokia has said

"The quality of work at Nokia derives from the understanding of individual qualities in people, caring for each other as well as the willingness to work together in a constructive way. In daily work at Nokia, respect for the individual means open communication, fairness, mutual trust and the acceptance of diversity."

Nokia Way, Values in action

◆ *Continuous learning.* There is a Finnish word, which is best translated as "humbleness." The Nokia culture denies that anyone ever gets past the ability to learn. All processes and activities could be done better if we only learn from each other, retain that information in the company and make it available to everyone else. The continuous learning culture is a dual concept – learning to improve the organization and learning to make individual progress. Nokia is sensitive to the fact that some great corporations have emerged, prospered and then, by making a mistake or, more likely, falling behind in some respect, died. Continuous learning is how Nokia intends to avoid such a fate.

Nokia has a robust induction process during which the values are explained. The recruits play games based on the values and are told lots of corporate war stories about them. During their annual review each employee answers questions about their performance based on the values. Lindsay Brooks, a human resources manager in Nokia Mobile phones in the UK, says "There is freedom to act, and the default option is trust. The constraints are found only in the values."

Nokia has said

"Nokia is an organisation in which individuals have a great deal of responsibility and freedom to make independent decisions. This, in turn, enables the company to respond quickly and serve its customers flexibly."

Nokia Way, Values in action

How then do they deal with incompetence if the values place so much emphasis on respect for the individual? Once again the values help. Respect for the individual includes openness and raising tricky issues rather than ducking them. It is hardly respect for an individual to keep them in a function in which they are struggling to be successful. Nokia admits a potential problem with the values when some individuals interpret them as "I can do what I want." But in the end it seems worth it to maintain the entrepreneur spirit.

Comment on – *reward systems*

There is nothing more demotivating for a member of a team, say a sales team, than to see a person rewarded when their actual performance has fallen short. Lots of managers let this happen when they feel that it is not entirely the person's fault that success was not achieved. The answer to that has to be – you give the reward when the person achieves the result by pure good luck. Why not deny it if they have had hard luck?

Where else does Nokia take a lead in getting the most out of its people and at the same time holding them in real respect? Employees make decisions on how to get the job done and have input to strategic decisions. The reward structure is egalitarian and skill based with everyone having some interest in the profits or shares of the business. The Nokia Connecting People Bonus Plan in 1999 paid the maximum five percent bonus to each participant in the scheme. They paid the maximum because the profits rose that year by 51 percent. They also have, at least in some parts of the company, a very effective little scheme that allows everyone in the company to claim £150, which they can spend on doing a NEW activity of their choice. This is fun, talked about constantly, and clearly acts as a highly effective motivator.

Ethical principles

Nokia aims for leadership here too. In terms of human rights they believe that it is in their long-term interests, as well as intrinsically right, to support complete freedom from discrimination. In any case, freedom of opinion and expression are an essential environment for the Nokia value of openness and straightforwardness.

Nokia has said

"Nokia is a global and multicultural company. The diversity of cultures and lifestyles is an important asset, enabling Nokia to better understand today's customers."

Nokia Way, Values in action

Whenever there is a hint of discrimination, for example, which the company allows can be hard to detect, the value of "not ducking issues" forces it out into the open so it can be dealt with.

Nokia has said

"With the diverse workforce we have at Nokia, it is imperative that we have a set of corporate values that are applicable worldwide. By utilizing these core values to guide our daily effort, we cannot help but be the innovators and leaders in the telecommunications industry. Our customers value our commitment to them and likewise we need to value our commitment to each other."

John Zanoff of Nokia Networks, USA

ASK YOURSELF

Here are eight points that Nokia tends to get right. How well does your organization do?

1 At recruitment they probe deeply to check out the fit of values of candidates.
2 Their flat structure allows quick communication through the organization.
3 They link their strategy to their people through their processes.
4 They make a process out of continuous learning.
5 Everyone knows the company strategy and can link it to their objectives.
6 Reward schemes give everyone a financial interest in the profitability of the business.
7 They encourage accountability and make sure that people know how their performance is measuring up against targets at all times.
8 They promote teamwork and an open, straightforward culture.

NOTES

1   *Fortune* Magazine, May 2000.

2   The Nokia Way.

---◆---

Four

GET YOUR HR STRATEGY RIGHT

---◆---

If Nokia thinks the secret of success is the attitude and motivation of individuals, then you would expect to see a strong human resources strategy linked closely to what the business is striving to achieve. Nokia does not disappoint.

TRANSFORMATION TO WORLD-CLASS HR

E very book or article you read on the topic of Nokia mentions the impressive way in which the new Nokia, post-1992, is able to transform itself with extraordinary speed. Transform is not too strong a word – just think of the transformation from unwieldy conglomerate in the 1980s to lean and mean mobile technology firm in the early 1990s.

Nokia has said

"Our future at Nokia depends on how well we use our collective imagination, developing products and services demanded by new realities. We cannot foresee the future, but we can prepare for it by taking a proactive stance and keeping our minds open. Regardless of what the future holds, we must play an active role in shaping these ends."

Jorma Ollila, Preface to Future Histories, *edited by Stephen McClelland*, 1997

What sort of human resources strategy backs up transformation, given the uncertain view of the future Ollila sees? It already has an impressively central role relative to many HR departments. It needs to be in the thick of the action. Nokia's phenomenal growth has thrown up immediate challenges for the company in the field of human resources. Rapid growth presents a management team with a multidimensional set of HR issues. All of these have to be developed in tandem with a coherent business strategy in order to keep the business in balance. Nokia's success in managing people through success has been a lesson to others. Nokia's people strategy is known within the business as the Nokia Way.

Comment on – *statements about company culture*
People operate better in an environment where they know what is
expected of them. An exposition of the company "way" is therefore
always helpful. It tells people clearly what they need to know about
what is required, although it is not necessarily a route map of how to
get there. The best statements of company culture grow over time
and represent more than just an expression of what the current chief
executive officer believes in.

Human resources in Nokia regarded the year 2000 as a year
of transition. At the end of this, HR is looking to provide a
world-class service supporting the overall business strategy
of the company. During the transition period they have a
lot to do. For example, they will implement the global HR
system to give some basic deliverables now and, perhaps more
importantly, to build the platform that will allow them to
deliver more into the future. Nokia believes that it still has a
long way to go to get to a world-class HR performance.

What is the nature of this transformation? It already keeps
managers up to date with its thinking and the strategy of those
at head office in Helsinki. In future it is expected to have a
central role in expressing the strategy in terms of the aspirations, letting managers know what they can expect to see
when these aspirations are fulfilled and providing a scorecard
mechanism, complete with very specific measures of success.

Comment on – *skills development*
Many managers see it as a luxury to send staff on training courses
for a post before they are actually doing the job, not least because of
the fear that it leads staff to believe that a promotion into the new
job is just round the corner. The logic of preparing people for their
next job is, however, overwhelming.

An internal Nokia document describes what Nokia managers can expect to see from a fully operational future HR strategy. Nokia's HR managers are essentially in place to ensure that business transformation takes place, when Nokia HQ wants it to, with a high degree of employee commitment. HR people are expected to support the business groups in handling transformation. They do this by setting measures of success, first of all through the response that managers make to HR surveys and feedback forms; secondly, by appointing HR "experts" in facilitating change.

Nokia has said

"We've just released the new Nokia Communicator 9210 but actually we're thinking several products ahead and hundreds of variations around each of them. You have to manage change because change is the fact of life, the constant, of our industry. We're thinking ten years ahead simply in order to stay slightly ahead of the others."

Mark Squire, Nokia Business Development Manager (UK)

LEARNING IS A PERSONAL THING TOO

Part of HR's role is not just respect for the individual, but support for the individual. Learning is a personal thing as well as an organizational process. People learn a lot from doing things and then planning further change with the mindset they developed through past experience.

Others have said

"It is through learning that managers really find out what a process such as managing change is all about. Getting managers to test the limits of their capabilities through learning new ways of operating not only pays off for the individual themselves but also for their organisations."

Managing Change, Ian Cunningham,
FT Handbook of Management, 1995

At the personal level, Nokia offers on its intranet the means whereby personnel can plan their own development program. They are offered training on every subject under the sun, from external courses through to internal technology-based learning The development is not only straightforward fact-based learning, but also in skills central to the Nokia values.

Nokia has said

"Remember that you are responsible for your development. Nokia supplies the opportunities, learning solutions, tools and methods for lifelong learning and employability."

No Limits, *Nokia, 2000*

Part of HR's role is not just respect for the individual, but support for the individual.

Thus we could say that at the organizational level Nokia retains its ability to metamorphose, while the creed of continuous learning mentioned earlier in this book centers round the individual and what is called "lifelong" learning. This concept is broader than continuous learning since it invites people to think that all of the situations they get into, whether inside or outside work, are opportunities to learn.

Nokia has said

"Our work and the technologies we deal with are changing very fast. Learning must be a life-long process and each of us is partly responsible for his or her own development and continuous learning."

Seppo Toivonen, Nokia employee, No Limits, Nokia 2000

That Nokia takes learning seriously is beyond doubt. Tim Burt in the *Financial Times* of March 1999 noted that the company has four learning centers catering to 50 countries each for new Nokians to undergo training and induction. This leads to mentor and tutoring programs that may last for months.

This induction is an important part of the HR strategy as it gives the company the opportunity to make sure that the Nokia values and methodologies are well understood.

GET THE BASICS RIGHT FOR THE FUTURE

One of the more mundane aims of Nokia human resources is to get the basics in place. The internal Nokia document mentioned earlier states that line managers will see basic HR products and services delivered with quality and operational effectiveness. Nokia managers can expect to "plug and play" from standardized platform solutions provided by HR. And they can expect both global and local information for HR purposes, such as employment rights, to be available to them online.

At the personal level, Nokia offers on its intranet the means whereby personnel can plan their own development program.

Others have said

"To improve, people must have a clear picture of where they are expected to be in terms of performance; the level of their current performance and how they need to go about bridging the gap between the two."

Appraisal, Brian Watling, FT Handbook of Management, *1995*

Watling's remark seems obvious until one looks at other companies who are victims of tenpin-bowling management, where management have put a curtain in front of the pins. As people hurl the ball down the alley through the curtain, their managers simply tell them how many they missed!

Nokia choose to implement external standards to make sure that everyone knows where they are and what is expected of them.

Nokia has said

"For example, we further developed our performance management initiative, Investing In People (IIP), under which all staff have regular discussions with their managers to set objectives and review skills and development needs."

No Limits, Nokia, 2000

All employees in the UK have had an IIP discussion within the last 12 months and all employees have a current development plan.

STANDARDIZE AND LOCALIZE

It is tempting to look at Nokia culture as still being essentially

Finnish. Tempting but mistaken. It is true that there are still Finns in many of the key positions in the company. But the rapid growth and the requirements of a worldwide company based on, amongst other things, many joint ventures and acquisitions means that there are important business units growing in many different local cultures. HR policy has to take this into account.

Comment on – globalization

Most companies have had the word "globalization" built into their language for some time, but few have completely understood just how much they have to empower the local people to make this happen.

Certainly, Nokia needs good HR and puts a lot of effort into facing up to the challenges of globalization. And there is a link to be made between the way Nokia tries to lead the world in defining and setting technology standards and the HR business model. Take technology standards first. A crucial benefit of market leadership is the hard-earned ability to set standards and Nokia is involved, mostly through its joint ventures and membership of technical working groups and committees, with the setting of numerous technical standards. Its membership of Symbian is an important example where Nokia, along with Motorola, Ericsson and the UK's Psion, is working on an operating system for a whole range of portable devices. If this operating system becomes the standard used by applications developers, then Nokia *et al.* are set to benefit. The opportunity is for the Symbian-produced operating system to be to portable devices what Windows is to the PC. In innovation terms as well, Nokia strives to gain competitive advantage by, for example, giving its people in R&D targets for the number of new patents they should register in any one year.

So how does the human resources strategy fit into this to set standards? Here, Nokia's organizational principles are:

◆ At the business unit level, it proposes HR practices to support the business strategy.

◆ At the geographic level, it seeks to understand and lead local HR practices and turn that knowledge into benefit, both locally and globally.

◆ At an external level, it has its own research and development monitoring world-class or best-practice HR products and services

Nokia calls this the flexibility balancing act. On one side of the equation is standardization, to give equal treatment and consistent reporting in a global sense, while on the other side is flexibility, necessary for localization of business groups, units and geographies.

FROM STRATEGY TO ACTION

HR strategy follows a well mapped-out route from plan to activity. It starts, of course, on the premise that key support for the business ambitions of Nokia, through partnering with management, will attract, retain, develop and motivate employees. From this standpoint, HR are able to work out how to organize themselves to reach their goals with the resources they have. This is then divided in three ways:

◆ roles and responsibilities;

◆ decision making responsibilities; and

◆ organizational models.

The role of HR in different locations is primarily, of course, to make sure that the implementation of global processes and concepts takes into account local legal requirements and the local business environment. They also manage the local service centers and services that are shared. They are also responsible for the roll out of the strategic plan, by setting their own local objectives and budgets. HR also take responsibility for recommending what should be global and what local, and for ensuring that Nokia remains at the leading edge of best HR practice.

RECRUITMENT AND RETENTION

All HR areas are important to business success, but recruitment has been critical to Nokia's continued success. It's not easy to recruit sometimes, with so many other things going on as the company develops. And for Nokia, it's not just about whether a candidate can do a particular job, but whether he of she can do it within a rapidly changing environment. Nokia overcomes this problem because it is not just looking for people who understand the technology but also for people who can apply the company's values and not just worry about how they fit into the company's hierarchy.

Keeping hold of staff is at least as challenging and hence staff motivation is also a key issue. Many companies offer share options to quality staff as a cheap and cash-free way of keeping them interested in the fortunes of the company and Nokia has its own incentivising employee share option schemes. The expansion of the market is a major element of the incentive to keep people with Nokia. The company has no particular hierarchy and so in a fast-growing company, you have to move people around to get experience of different parts of the business. As long as the company has done its job in recruiting the right sorts of people for the company at the early stage then new challenges and responsibility are the greatest form of motivation.

ASK YOURSELF

Here are the five points that Nokia tends to get right. How well does your organization do?

1 The HR strategy is derived from and aligned with the business strategy.

2 HR strategy has an aim to make Nokia the employer of choice in an environment where there is an increasing shortage of skilled people and the competition for such people is intense and becoming more so.

3 The closeness of the business strategy to HR helps Nokia to have the skills in place before they need them, rather than discovering the need for them in a crisis.

4 HR helps to produce an environment that welcomes change, and allows the business to transform itself dramatically without losing a significant amount of employee commitment.

5 The HR policy is driven by the needs of Nokia's customers.

---◆---

Five

BRAND FOR THE WORLD – AND THE INDIVIDUAL

---◆---

This chapter traces Nokia's approach to market segmentation and divining customer's future needs. It also compares Nokia's methods of brand management with traditional theories and the Nokia claim to be breaking new ground in its approach to globalization.

SEGMENTATION THE NOKIA WAY

Many companies believe that talking about market segmentation is a simple process. Take this dictum: "There is no such thing as a product if there is no market for it, and there is no such thing as a market unless you have a product to sell into it. Think only in product markets – segments of the market that will buy a particular product of yours."[1]

It's sensible enough stuff, but perhaps a little one-dimensional. Selling more mobile phones to more people is more than a concentration of to whom one should sell new product features, or even how to find new product features to suit a given gender, age or income.

Nokia believes that the old style of market segmentation does not go far enough. Segmentation is not a one-off activity. People at Nokia instead try to think about market segmentation as a continuous evolution of consumer psychology, based around the needs of the individual.

Nokia has said

"We need to understand how consumers live their lives, what are their attitudes, their lifestyle and beliefs. It is the individual value systems that we are seeking to understand."[2]

Nigel Litchfield, senior vice-president, Nokia Mobile Phone in Asia Pacific

Nigel Litchfield believes that if you divide up markets in a manner more convenient to the marketing department than the consumer, you will never pinpoint psychological changes in consumer attitudes towards mobile technology. Information, such as demographics and geographical spread, is of course important to segmentation, but is just a means to an end rather than the end of the story. No amount of neat and tidy market dividing will help you to sell more mobile phones (or anything else for that matter) unless you get to the psychology of what people want and why they want it – the drivers behind any sale.

Nokia has said

"The most important thing is to understand the key drivers of the consumers, such as what motivates them and excites them. This enables us to truly connect with the consumers."[3]

Nigel Litchfield, senior vice-president, Nokia Mobile Phone in Asia Pacific

Looking at consumer psychology is one step ahead of discovering consumer attitudes. Here's why. Nokia thinks that understanding end-users in the evolving mobile market requires a "holistic" approach (which means that an understanding of the whole system of attitudes is needed). Questions such as "Would you use the messaging function?" or "Would you give a mobile phone to your daughter if calls were prepaid?" take Nokia only so far in understanding their customers. In order to go the extra mile down the road, Nokia must ask questions such as:

◆ Why do you communicate?

◆ With whom do you communicate with your mobile phone?

◆ What are the benefits of your mobile phone?

These are questions that the consumer cannot answer with a curt "yes" or "no." The answers reveal far more about how the consumer thinks in making his or her decisions.

Here is what Jorma Ollila says about the company's approach to mobility in the work place.

Nokia has said

"Where is economic growth being created? It is being created in those spots and those spaces, industries and companies where there is productivity enhancement. So it's the rise in productivity which is driving the way people want to communicate, work and spend their lives."[4]

Jorma Ollila, Capital Markets Day in Dallas, December 1999

Ollila's vision of "productivity enhancements" and the way in which it is applied in various market segments in the Nokia framework leads to greater personalization of the product. Different people need different things for different reasons. "There are unique clusters of attitudes but not unique product needs," explains Litchfield. He believes that the understanding of this principle, perhaps more than anything else, has put Nokia into the forefront of its market.

Nokia has said

"We believe that those days when mobile phone makers could offer only one mobile phone that serves everyone's needs are over. Personalising phones, with for example colour and ring tone, will increasingly be done ... [and] the use of wireless application ... gives end users different ways of accessing data communication and storing information."[5]

Nigel Litchfield, senior vice-president, Nokia Mobile Phone in Asia Pacific

An example of personalization is the hook-up that Nokia has with EMI Music Publishing. It has an agreement for EMI's publishing catalog to be used for customized downloadable ring tones. Consumers get the additional feature of using well-known songs, television and film themes as their ring tones, by downloading them from the Internet site, Club Nokia. Possibly as important, is the fact that Nokia has anticipated that ring tones can also be provided for promotional purposes and hence could in future be sponsored.

Comment on – *personalization*

Personalization of any product is only available if there is sufficient variation built into the design of the product. Inventing variations is a creative task and is only made possible by encouraging people to think laterally about what customers want from the product.

When something you want becomes unique and personal to you in the way it looks, sounds and performs, it effectively becomes a fashion accessory.

WAP technology will play a massive part in personalization. It has been estimated that there will be nearly half a billion Internet users by 2003. The Nokia WAP (wireless application protocol) phone, the 7110 model launched in 1999, will play its part in accelerating this growth by increasing the potential for the personalization of needs. "Giving consumers access to the Internet through mobile phones will lead to a revolution in the way [individual] people access information," finishes Litchfield.

The approach to personalization has also opened some unexpected avenues of benefit for Nokia. When something you want becomes unique and personal to you in the way it looks, sounds and performs, it effectively becomes a fashion accessory, a reflection of lifestyle as well as the means to perform a task. This is why in 1999 Nokia launched the 8210 phone in co-operation with the fashion industry. It took part in the Paris Fashion Show in both 1999 and 2000. Pekka Rantala sums this Nokia Way of segmenting markets rather well in this context.

Nokia has said

"We are very happy to participate in Paris fashion week. Our experience last year was very positive, and we intend to continue our involvement in various lifestyle related events and activities. The success of our fashion category has proved that in today's world, mobile phones are much more than communications tools only; they are accessories that enhance the lifestyles and express the tastes and personalities of individuals everywhere."[6]

Pekka Rantala, vice-president, Nokia Mobile Phone, Europe and Africa

THE STRENGTH OF NOKIA'S BRAND

In a speech in 1999 to analysts and other financial commentators in the Capital Markets Day in Dallas, Jorma Ollila spoke of Nokia's passion for its brand management.

Nokia has said

"Let's look at brand – its something we have worked on really consistently and even single-mindedly since 1991. We have put a lot of energy into it, a lot of thinking into it and, of course, some money and investment."[7]

Jorma Ollila

The money and investment seem to have paid off. It is always good to get independent corroboration of a company's claim to have a great brand and Nokia recently got it from its position in the Interbrand year-2000 survey of the 75 leading brands (see Key Facts box). Interbrand studied 150 brands using the following selection criteria:

◆ The brands had to be truly global.

◆ Interbrand identified main categories (e.g. cars, alcohol, tobacco, leisure, etc.) and determined the leading brand in each category. "Brands were thus excluded from the study on the basis of a lack of a clear category leadership."[8]

◆ There had to be sufficient marketing and financial data available in order to prepare a reasonable valuation.

And this from a brand that only began to go wholeheartedly into the mobile telecommunications market in 1992. At that time many people thought Nokia was a Japanese company (a fact that many inside Nokia believe was actually a plus). How has this phenomenal growth in brand awareness happened, and more importantly what can the rest of us learn from it?

Comment on – *local empowerment*

There is a delicate balance to be made between global branding and local variation. This is easier to achieve if you remember that the product is only part of the overall brand image. Concentrating only on the globalization of the key factors leaves the country managers free to personalize within their own cultures.

Let us make a connection first between the Nokia approach to market segmentation and theories of brand management.

KEY FACTS

Here are the top companies emerging from the Interbrand survey. Those rated above Nokia are included for comparison purposes

Rank	Brand	Brand value 2000 ($m)	Brand value 1999 ($m)	% change	Market capitalisation ($m)
1	Coca-Cola	72,537	83,845	-13%	142,163
2	Microsoft Windows	70,197	56,654	24%	420,992
3	IBM	53,184	43,781	21%	194,236
4	Intel	39,049	30,021	30%	447,719
5	Nokia	38,528	20,694	86%	239,828

There are two fundamental approaches to branding. The traditional "product plus" approach which sees branding as an addition to the product. The definition given in Philip Kotler's classic textbook, *Marketing Management*, typifies this approach: "A brand name is a name, term, sign, symbol or design or a combination of these, which is intended to identify the goods or services of one group of sellers and differentiate them from those of competitors."[9] From this perspective the brand is applied once all the product development issues are settled. Basically the brand then gives the consumer the security that the source of the product is tried and tested. What it gives to the manufacturer is protection against a competitor passing off.

Nokia's approach to branding, like its approach to market segmentation, is part of the second "holistic" school. Chris Styles and Tim Ambler write of the holistic approach, "This regards the product as just one element of the brand – a single component of the marketing mix alongside price, promotion and distribution. The product is only part of what the consumer experiences of the total brand. The brand from this perspective is the promise of a bundle of attributes that someone buys and that provides satisfaction."[10]

We need one other definition – that for a "value chain" – if we are to understand Nokia's take on branding. According to the *FT Handbook of Management*, the value chain is a firm's co-ordinated set of activities to satisfy customer needs, starting with relationships with suppliers and procurement, going through production, selling and marketing, and ending up with delivery to the customer. Each stage of the value chain is linked with the next stage, and looks forward to the customer's needs. Each link in the value chain must seek competitive advantage: it must either be lower cost than the corresponding link in competing firms, or add more value by superior quality or differentiated features.[11]

Nokia has said

"There are four stages in our value chain. First of all the development of a market leading application from Nokia or a strategic partner or from both of us working together. Second, we start to tightly integrate or 'harden' what exactly the product is, by producing purpose built hardware and getting the right operating system. Thirdly, we put great emphasis on the rapid deployment of the product. Finally, we have a principle of 'first call, final resolution.' This means that if there's something the customer needs to know or can't understand about the product he can sort out the issue with us with one phone call. We won't pass a technical problem onto one of our suppliers – Nokia deals with it. The buck stops here."

Julie Parrish, VP marketing and public affairs,
Nokia Internet Communications

Ollila and his Nokia colleagues explain that you cannot understand the Nokia Way of branding without knowing that it is crucial at every stage in the value chain. This is not just a matter of screwing the suppliers to give the customer the cheapest deal, although obviously margins are an important consideration. All the partners in the chain, from suppliers to distributors, gain from working with and for the Nokia brand. The company's image of ethical trading is, says Nokia, as much a part of the brand as the product itself because it is part of the way in which the product comes across to the customer.

> The company's image of ethical trading is, says Nokia, as much a part of the brand as the product itself because it is part of the way in which the product comes across to the customer.

GLOBALIZATION THE NOKIA WAY

The Finnish market has been a useful playground for Nokia in building its global brand and giving pointers to future consumer attitudes. Nokia's understanding and insight into consumers has a lot to do with the mutual impact that Finns and Nokia have had on one another. This has provided insights into how customer needs may develop overseas in the future. With its near saturation level of usage among Finns, mobile technology has had more impact on the culture of business in Finland than anywhere else.

For example, in Finland senior managers routinely put their mobile phone number on their cards. In the US and the rest of Europe, a senior manager is still more likely than not to have on his or her business card a switchboard number that will be answered by an administrative assistant who will filter the calls to go through to the boss.

Others have said

"In the USA you're not supposed to call your boss until they call you. People find it degrading if their subordinate calls them. In Finland, if I want to be important I keep my phone on all the time, so I'll be available when decisions need to be made. In most other countries people believe that mobile phones give them power because of who they can call conveniently. Here, people think mobile phones give them power because of who can phone them."[12]

Risto Linturi, principal research fellow, Helsinki Telephone Corporation

In the US, the big boss will probably be too important to be called directly by all but the bravest junior. But the Finnish experience at least gives an experience of possible future trends in other countries.

This is important because any company building a global brand needs a philosophy whereby subsidiary companies are somehow simultaneously consistent with their global HQ, but also relatively autonomous in making changes when it becomes clear that a trend in the domestic market may not work overseas. This is true for any other multinational company, but think how much more true it must be for Nokia. With a tiny market share derived from its home country and with ever-shortening product life cycles, it has been critical for Nokia to get the balance right between central control and local culture.

Another crucial aspect of Nokia's brand building across the world lies in moving quickly. Here is a short extract from

Nokia's annual report *No Limits*, which recorded just some of the expansion of Nokia's manufacturing worldwide in 1999:

Nokia has said

"Nokia's operations in Fort Worth, Texas are increasing mobile phone capacity ...

"Also during the first half of 2000 mobile phone manufacturing facilities in Brazil are being expanded, and the mobile phone plant in Mexico is expected to be ready for additional production.

"Construction of the mobile phone manufacturing and distribution centre in Komarom, Hungary proceeded well ...

"Investments were also made at the two existing mobile phone joint ventures in China, and at the plants in Finland and Germany. The base station factory in Suzhou, China started operations in early 2000.

"At the end of 1999, Nokia's global production comprised 12 infra-structure manufacturing facilities in 5 countries and 10 mobile phone manufacturing facilities in 8 countries."[13]

No Limits

In one article, the business author Karl Moore suggests that in the emerging global economy most subsidiaries have lost strategic decision-making power to their multinational head-quarters, while relatively few have gained a larger global role thanks to deliberate decentralisation.[14] Many of those central-izing decisions have typically taken control of which markets to compete for, which products to introduce, what type of manager to hire and where to locate the research and develop-ment and manufacturing parts of the firm. While this has cleared the decks for global strategy and global competitive moves, it has often resulted in demotivated subsidiary teams and a considerable drop in overall corporate learning.

Comment on – *working with other cultures*

The concept of the internal customer is important when working with other cultures. If you regard the departments in subsidiary companies as somehow subservient to head office, then your company has a real problem. If you look on them as internal customers then you are already half way to understanding their culture and producing the best product for the local market.

This is the opposite of the Nokia Way of doing business. For Nokia, the key is dependence on the leadership of subsidiary company managers and the development of world-class competencies no matter what their provenance. For example, Nokia in the UK has built up its R&D capabilities over the years to the point where its facility now has global responsibility for important lines of product.

Nokia has said

"To date, we have research and development centres in 14 countries. These facilities allow us to adapt our products to meet local market requirements. But far more valuable in our rapidly changing world is that we really do our research from start to finish at all sites in parallel. This way we have access to the best talent the world has to offer, and to share the latest knowledge around the world."[14]

Juhani Kuusi, senior vice-president, Nokia Research Centre

ASK YOURSELF

Here are the five points that Nokia tends to get right. How well does your organization do?

1 Understands exactly why customers buy their products and not just who they are.
2 Realizes the importance of product personalization.
3 Recognizes that the product is just one aspect of the overall brand.
4 Gives real autonomy to its country subsidiaries.
5 Moves quickly to put its global plans into place.

NOTES

1 Bruce, Andrew (1997) *Creating a Market Sensitive Culture*, Pitman Publishing.

2 *Star Malaysia*, July 1999.

3 See note 2.

4 Tape of Capital Markets Day Nokia held in December 1999.

5 See note 2.

6 Nokia press release, 2000.

7 See note 4.

8   Interbrand Criteria and Methodology for Brands Survey, www.interbrand.com, 2000.

9   Kotler, Philip (1993) *Marketing Management: Analysis, Planning and Control*, 8th edition, Prentice Hall, Englewood Cliffs, NJ.

10   Styles, Chris and Ambler, Tim (1995) Brand Management, *The FT Handbook of Management*.

11   Definition of Terms, *The FT Handbook of Management*, 1995.

12   *Wired*, September 1999.

13   Survey Mastering Global Business 4: How Subsidiaries Can be More than Bit Players, *Financial Times*, 1998.

14   *No Limits*, Nokia's annual report, 1999.

---◆---

Six

INNOVATE RELENTLESSLY, COMPETE REMORSELESSLY

---◆---

This chapter looks at what we can we learn from Nokia's apparent ability to innovate throughout its business and how it builds sustainable competitiveness through innovation.

DEALING WITH ADVERSITY

I t may seem odd to start a chapter about Nokia's reputation for innovation and competitiveness by referring to a bad patch that the company hit in 1995. Even so, it is worth examining one crisis – a huge distribution bottleneck – that the company faced in that year. At a time when first-class innovation and clever marketing were the twin engines driving phenomenal demand for Nokia handsets, the logistics side of the company was failing to get the product out of the factory and into the global distribution chain at anything like the required rate. This caused very big losses. Sean Faughan, telecommunications analyst at JP Morgan in London, puts it like this. "The share price collapsed just as Nokia was making the transition to a high volume producer of handsets." Yet somehow Nokia recovered its respectability in the market place in double-quick time. "Their recovery later on in 1996," says Faughan, "was quite remarkable at a time when many people were writing them off."[1]

Comment on – *re-engineering*

How quickly can your organization reshape itself? This comes down, in part at least, to creating an expectation that peoples' jobs and organization will change regularly. Being change-orientated allows the organization to change without losing focus. It is possible to change an organization dramatically without even attracting the attention, for example, of the people involved in producing the next version of the product.

How did Nokia move from disaster to triumph in such a short space of time? We can find the answer in the way Nokia takes on global innovation. First of all, nobody at Nokia got shot for the mismatch of supply and demand. The absence of a blame culture allowed people to look forward rather than find excuses. Key Nokia staff formed into task forces to look at what was needed to be done. Everyone in the company was made aware of what was going on and was encouraged to look at their own potential contribution to the way ahead, no matter what their particular role in distribution.[2]

... what started as an embarrassment in the eyes of outsiders became an opportunity to find an innovative solution which would make the company stronger in the long term.

The solution adopted also reflects the Nokia Way of doing things. This was no patchwork solution to get things moving again, but a complete review of the company's overall distribution strategy. In other words, what started as an embarrassment in the eyes of outsiders became an opportunity to find an innovative solution which would make the company stronger in the long term. What did they do? The taskforce recommended Nokia's swift introduction of new logistics software as the key to recovery, as well as the prime factor in the company's continuing expansion. Faughan notes: "it enabled them to control their inventories and their cost of sales and distribution. That is one reason why they have such strong margins now."

The point of this story is that it is to help you, the reader, understand that Nokia's concept of innovation is not limited to product and services. Rather, innovation is ingrained throughout the whole ethos of the organization, in every nook and cranny of its planning and operation.

WHY INNOVATION IS LIKE PLAYING IN AN ORCHESTRA

Before the watershed of 1995, of course, came the nadir of 1992. It set the tone with which Nokia's leader, Jorma Ollila, sought to change the company – if you change people, corporate change will follow. The transformation is described by Justin Fox in *Fortune*.

Others have said

"The phone business had become paralysed by low morale and disorganization. And Ollila, it turns out, has a gift for straightening out such problems. He hit the factory floor in Salo, about an hour west of Helsinki, to listen to workers and tell them his plans. He streamlined an organisation that had gotten terribly tangled trying to prepare for the then new European digital cellular standard called GSM. It was Ollila's defining career moment. 'That was my university,' he says now. To a few key members of Nokia's board, it marked him down as the company's potential saviour."[4]

Justin Fox

All commentators agree that Ollila is a brilliant team builder. He has been described by many as a hard task master, and he certainly looks and sounds driven by a huge determination to find the right plan and make it happen.[5] "He is extremely demanding and can be very rude if he is not satisfied" one senior Nokia manager confesses.[6]

Comment on – *management style*

A way of running a business that treats people with decency need not reduce the demands made on them. It is not possible to combine new and innovative thinking with total comfort for those doing jobs. No organization can afford this and people working for it usually understand that.

Hearing speeches made by Ollila more recently reminds you that whatever the topic he is addressing, he will come back to overall strategy and refer to the Nokia Way as the vehicle through which the company will deliver. An interesting example of this came at a Nokia presentation at the Capital Markets Day in Dallas in 1999. Ollila explained how he believed that the company would use innovation to stay ahead. He took his starting point as the vision for the future they had arrived at some time previously and still current today.

Nokia has said

"I think we were among the first ones to really put meat around the bones of what is needed to become successful in this new era. What we said was that we want to take a leading, brand-recognised role in creating the mobile information society by combining a mobility and Internet service and stimulating the creation of new services ... we feel we can bring unique solutions in the area of human technology and that's very much part of our plan ... How are we going to do that? We are going to do that by being an orchestra, by being the market maker."

Jorma Ollila, Capital Markets Day, Dallas 1999

This metaphor is interesting. Nokia is the orchestra, and Nokia people come over very much as part of an orchestra. In his autobiography *Writing Home*, the playwright Alan Bennett gives an insight into different attitudes amongst team members. He differentiates musicians in an orchestra from actors. In the first case:

> "What is striking about the musicians is their total absence of self-importance."

He describes how the musicians play a piece and then discuss amongst themselves as to how it might be improved. They make suggestions for each other directly, not via the director. Anyone is invited to comment, their views noted and in some cases adopted when they go to repeat the piece. According to Bennett this would be impossible with actors.

Fortune magazine reported that Nokia's market share in mobile phones in 1999 was 27 percent.

In the reality of business life, however, Nokia managers don't manage everyone in the same way. Some of the team they can easily encourage to be musicians, and some, sometimes the most talented, will always be actors. But the orchestra analogy is still valid. In most teams in other companies, the egos of individuals get in the way of innovation. In the Nokia culture, people encourage openness and constructive criticism and tend to be very laid back and good listeners.

> **In the Nokia culture, people encourage openness and constructive criticism and tend to be very laid back and good listeners.**

KEY FACTS ON PRODUCT INNOVATION

No Limits reports:

1 Nokia has more than 17,000 in research and development
2 Expenditure on R&D has grown by more than 50 percent per year over the last two years
3 In 1998 Nokia made over 700 patent applications. This increased to over 1000 in 1999
4 The number of invention reports went up from 2000 to 3000 in the same period

INNOVATION IS A CONTINUOUS PROCESS ...

At Nokia, innovation in the mobile information society is more about the ongoing application of a plan than it is about technology. It is extraordinary how many companies still fail to carry through strategies for innovation. Many managers speak of a strategic plan as being correct in many of its aspirations and assumptions, but incorrect in others at "at least as far as my subsidiary/customer is concerned?"

Comment on – *using individual initiative*

Connecting a departmental strategy to an overall corporate statement is undoubtedly good for business but usually carries with it a danger of stifling individual talent. Never use corporate strategy to gag or stifle talent in the organization. Look for the link between strategic plans, but be prepared to alter more senior strategies when someone has a go at a better idea. You never know at what level in the organization the next big idea will come from.

Thinking such as this makes different parts of the organization pull in different directions, only coming together, and then in a crisis and with great difficulty, when a customer gets upset. When a sales team is dealing with a complaint from a customer, for example, the former usually go directly or indirectly to the people responsible for the offending product and pushes the requirements of an individual customer at the production level. The innovation team, R&D or manufacturing, then has to decide whether or not to include new software or product to meet this need. If it doesn't, the company is plainly letting down a customer. But if it does, it may later find that it is letting down several more for some unforeseen reason. The dilemma is compounded by the fact that any plan for innovation never remains static if the industry is changing fast. And there is no industry that is changing faster than that of mobile technologies.

... WHICH LEADS TO GREATER COMPETITIVENESS

Ollila maintains that innovation must be reviewed continuously. That way you do not become stuck with something that is already out of date, simply because the plan itself is out of date.[7] Every plan has its merits, but ultimately is secondary to the business strategy which, of course, is driven entirely by customer requirements. Ollila concedes that this process is very challenging because you need to make a continuous

> This continuous reassessment to innovation extends throughout the way Nokia Way of working.

adjustment. "Challenging" can mean "infuriating" at times but, he says, the plan must not differentiate or separate strategy from the organization or from the implementation processes.

This continuous reassessment to innovation extends throughout the way Nokia Way of working. Ollila says that he is often asked what sort of acquisition they are about to make at a particular time.

Nokia has said

"I think the first comment I would make is we do not have an acquisition strategy; we do have a business strategy where acquisitions play a certain role."

Jorma Ollila, Capital Markets Day, Dallas 1999

He then goes on to say that acquisitions will be in small- and medium-sized technology companies with a like-minded approach to innovation. This, he says, will ensure Nokia's continued competitiveness.

So far, then, we have concentrated on the processes needed to ensure that your innovation meets the customers' needs:

1   Close attention to the customer in terms of lifestyle as well as desirable functionality of products and services.

2   Empowering the innovators to go down tracks that think may be interesting without having to prove in advance they are not a red herring.

3   Not shooting anyone when some project research turns out actually to be a red herring

4   Creating flexible plans, with continuous review built in to the innovation process itself.

5   Making available, on a global basis, the experience of all the teams involved in the process of innovation.

But the application of innovation carries with it one massive caveat – only if the end user accepts the new innovation, improves the way he or she communicates, works or relaxes will it be accepted. Competitiveness means more than good innovation. It means getting people to try out Nokia innovation in preference to the alternatives.

It is therefore perhaps not surprising to see what the most important thing about competitiveness is according to Ollila.

Nokia has said

"A key competitive factor is the brand. When new technologies are introduced many people initially feel slightly uneasy about it. Do I need it? Will I be able to understand it? The strong and recognised brand translates into credibility. Consumers are more likely to trust an old brand when it comes to new solutions or innovations, other than an unknown producer."

Jorma Ollila, Capital Markets Day, Dallas 1999

INNOVATION THROUGH DESIGN

Innovative design has been agreed by everyone to be a major competitive plus.

Others have said

"So how does Nokia do it? Shrewd marketing and clever engineering are important parts of the answer. Its latest model, a sleek, silver-coloured gadget known as the 8810, is in such high demand that it is trading at close to 50 percent above its recommended retail price on London's black market. "People just get excited about their phones: they do interesting things. Nokia has tapped a fashion niche."[8]

Tim Burt and Greg McIvor

But that was back in 1998, have they kept it up? They certainly have not changed the continuous process of innovative design and re-design. In October 1999, *The Economist* reported that while Nokia R&D managers still get a lot of fun out of pulling a new mock up of a video phone or suchlike out of their pockets, they still have a lot of selling to do internally if they are to be able to take this to the stage of manufacture. The system of "internal start-ups" demands that people who have come up with a good idea are expected to produce a business model and then move from the laboratory to a business unit to try to turn it into reality.

Comment on – R&D spend

Lord Leverhulme once said, "Half the money I spend on advertising is wasted, and the trouble is I don't know which half." In the R&D context prescient managers acknowledge that at least half the R&D budget will be wasted. Yet R&D is the only sure-fire way to keep up with the fickle tastes of customers.

This brings the business unit, who will have to make and sell the product, into the process at an early stage. They also process quality into each part of the design and manufacturing process. So well do they tackle quality issues that they won the European Quality Award in the Large Business category in 2000, the first year they took part. The European Foundation for Quality Management, who present the award, looked for the highest level of commitment to improving their business practices and competitiveness. This year's winners were selected on the basis of a site visit from a team of assessors. During their one week visit the team met approximately 500 people in nine different Nokia sites. They chose Nokia from a short list of 23 finalists representing different industries from 13 different countries.

We will leave the last word on innovation and competitiveness to Ollila. Notice how the topic is specific, but the message still the usual general one – know your quarry.

Nokia has said

"When we look at the development of our products in the future the key word for our competitiveness is personalisation. People will not only be able to pick up products or look at other mobile phone models that have the look and feel. They will also to choose the features and services that they personally want and need. Personalisation can and will take place in three following dimensions – design, function and service."

Jorma Ollila, Capital Markets Day, Dallas 1999

ASK YOURSELF

Here are the five points that Nokia tends to get right. How well does your organization do?

1 Nokia people can connect what they are doing with what the market wants in the future.
2 Nokia acknowledge that you cannot sell innovation in volume without brand recognition.
3 The amounts of money invested in innovation and R&D reflect the challenge of life cycles in technology.
4 Nokia encourages people to have a go.
5 They link the product developers with the product manufacturers and sellers at an early stage in a project by making the innovators sell their ideas internally.

NOTES

1   *Financial Times*, Tim Burt and Greg McIvor, October, 1998.

2   Various articles and reports.

3   See note 1.

4   Fox, Justin (2000) "Nokia's Secret Code," *Fortune* magazine, May.

5   See note 2.

6   See note 1.

7   Tape of Capital Markets Day, Dallas, TX December 1999.

8   See note 1.

Seven

TREAT SUPPLIERS WITH RESPECT

Suppliers are a significant part of the Nokia story. This chapter shows how Nokia pushes its suppliers hard but is loyal to those who meet its requirements.

BEGIN WITH THE END IN MIND

The importance of good purchasing and supply management cannot be emphasized too strongly for any global firm. Every step, from the identification of the need for purchased goods or services through to their reception and use, provides an opportunity to reduce cost and improve efficiency and effectiveness. To achieve this requires implementing well-functioning systems and developing a high degree of professional competence.

Comment on – *suppliers*

Just as with internal people, so with suppliers. You can treat them well without lowering the demands that you make on them.

Jorma Ollila certainly agrees. He says that when you look at the parts of the value chain in the cellular mobile industry you get benefits of economies of scale in every part of the value chain starting from supplier relationships, technology platforms, productization all the way to the consumer and the demand chain.

This thought is echoed by the gurus:

Others have said

"In years past, manufacturers were the drivers of the supply chain – managing the pace at which products were manufactured and distributed. Today, customers are calling the shots and manufacturers are scrambling to meet customer demands for options/styles/features, quick order fulfilment and fast delivery.

"Manufacturing quality – a long time competitive differentiator – is approaching parity across the board, so meeting customers' specific demands for product delivery has emerged as the next critical opportunity for competitive advantage. Companies that learn how to improve management of their supply chain will become the next success stories in the global market place."

Supply-Chain Council

USE BOTH THE STICK AND THE CARROT WITH SUPPLIERS

Where does that take us in terms of suppliers? Fundamentally, the consideration of the end-user has the twin effect of Nokia making heavy demands on their suppliers, whilst realizing that when a suppler has met such demand – and so made the customer happy – then that supplier needs to be rewarded and looked after. They expect their suppliers to be as dedicated to innovation as they are. They expect them to understand the value chain and what their operation adds to it. They have moved from making everything themselves to partnerships and high levels of outsourcing. They negotiate for exclusivity as well as, or perhaps in preference to, cost. Put simply, they will pay a bit more for the exclusive right to a technology or an application.

Nokia has said

"We experiment with hundreds of variations on a product in its development. Our suppliers are fine with all the tinkering and adjustments. They, like us, are wanting to see how far they can push the technology. As long as we are all working to the same basic protocols, its merely creating variations around a single theme."

Mark Squires, Nokia Business Development Manager (UK)

Just as we have seen how the Nokia approach pays benefits in terms of innovation, customers and Nokia people, equally the openness with which Nokia approaches its suppliers pays back over and over again. Justin Fox[1] explains that the new approach to suppliers goes back to the beginning, when outside suppliers were included in the team of researchers, designers, marketers and manufacturing types around the world that developed the phone for all three digital standards in 1991.

Nokia has said

"The means of distribution is obviously very important. Just as we have to think very carefully about tailoring our products to meet the personalised demands of our customer, so we also have to continuously think – and then re-think – the way in which we push the product out to the market."

Mark Squires, Nokia Business Development Manager (UK)

It happened again when the logistics task forces in 1995 revolutionized the distribution system in 1995 and solved the bottleneck in a breathtaking six months – again with the help of its suppliers. And supplier co-operation continues. The Nokia Way smoothes the boundaries between customer and supplier and encourages co-operation through frank and open interchange of ideas, problems and potential solutions.

Others have said

"Nokia is a delight to deal with. They are good listeners, and when they decide that you have something to offer, they seem to make it their business to make your offering as beneficial to both sides as they possibly can.

"A small, but important, example: if for some reason they fail to make a payment on the due date, no matter who you talk to, line managers or the administrative function, everyone seems genuinely concerned that they have made a mistake, and hard working in their efforts to put it right."[2]

Chief executive, supplier of software

The Nokia attention to the environment is something of a two-edged sword to their suppliers. Nokia makes heavy demands on suppliers to make sure that any product or packaging they supply to the company is produced in line with good environmental practice. On the other hand Nokia is happy to supply resources and information to companies to assist them to examine their current methods and look for more environmentally sound procedures. "In any case the Nokia value that says 'Don't shirk the issue' forces us to take a view on the performance of a supplier in this regard and to face them with the problem where this is needed."[3]

> Nokia is happy to supply resources and information to companies to assist them to examine their current methods and look for more environmentally sound procedures.

Comment on – *the environment and the brand*
Adverse publicity about the way a company treats the planet affects the brand image as much as any product problem. Some of the worst brand collapses are concerned with environmental complacency – just ask the oil companies.

According to Greg McIvor of the *Financial Times Exporter*, Nokia wrote to all suppliers and sub-contractors urging them to convert to Euro pricing as soon as possible.[4] Only partly was this to ease their own entry into the new currency, partly also it was a genuine attempt to alert suppliers to the need to prepare early for a new opportunity that could turn into a threat if action were not taken.

Their conviction that everyone had to make the effort to change early was seen as part of their team work with their suppliers.

PARTNERSHIP SOURCING – THE WAY FORWARD

The traditional relationship between purchasers and suppliers has been adversarial, often built around a lack of trust and fuelled by insecurity. Increasingly, this conventional and limited relationship is being replaced by "partnership sourcing" the process of building strong, lasting and mutually beneficial relationships between customers and suppliers. Initially developed by large multinationals as a means of improving quality and lowering the cost of purchases from smaller suppliers, partnership sourcing is now gaining wider use and growing in importance as a weapon in improving organizational competitiveness.

Comment on – *partnership*

If there is a single issue that separates the ideal partnership relationship from the real one, it is the presence or absence of joint forward-planning sessions. You cannot have a partnership where one partner's strategy is hidden from the other party.

Nokia is a keen advocate of this approach. Illustrations of Nokia's attempts to do this abound. The ethos of teamwork and task forces easily extends to teams outside the company's own people. The push for leadership in emerging markets is accompanied by encouragement in the countries themselves to set up supply chains to service Nokia and others. In 1999, China exported more than US\$ 600 million worth of components for Nokia Group use.

Nokia has said

"We will integrate China into the global picture. Purchasing components for the group's global use is the most efficient way."

Folke Ahlback, chairman of the board, Nokia China

EXPERIENCE COUNTS

Perhaps the varied nature of the businesses historically in the Nokia group could be responsible for the company's quick, and seemingly more simple than others, move into an understanding of managing an effective value chain. Remember that the company's roots lie in toilet paper and engineering.

Others have said

"Fast-moving consumer goods markets have long recognised the importance of logistics, especially through the distribution of goods through retail channels. Often, however, it is not recognised that the supply side to the manufacturer offers similar opportunities. Durables are rapidly following down the same path with some products increasingly resembling fashion items and others behaving as if they were commodities. In capital equipment markets the switch to customer order-driven processes is more complete and the timescale may be extended. However, the cost of failure can be enormous."[5]

Douglas Macbeth, Logistics Management

Nokia is in all the markets that Macbeth mentions. Their durables side has had to keep up to date with the fashion industry, while their networks side has to work within the capital investment programs of its suppliers and customers. Each can teach the other something and the Nokia Way is the device by which senior managers can make sure that this cross-functional learning happens.

ASK YOURSELF

Here are the five points that Nokia tends to get right. How well does your organization do?

1 They understand every component of their value chain.
2 They look for value added from all aspects of the chain, well beyond the manufacturing area.
3 They look for places that the Nokia brand can add value to the work of others in the chain.
4 They put reality behind the pious claim to build "working partnerships" with their suppliers.
5 They pull suppliers into the task forces set up to search for innovation or solve problems.

NOTES

1   *Fortune* magazine, 2000.

2   In conversation.

3   Lindsay Brooks, in conversation.

4   Survey – *Financial Times Exporter*, September 1998.

5   Logistics Management, Douglas Macbeth, FT Handbook of Management, 1995.

Eight

LET'S GET TOGETHER

There are many reasons why companies form joint ventures and alliances and Nokia seems to be an enthusiastic advocate of all of them. Nokia's leaders see joint ventures and alliances as a thoroughly desirable fact of life, rather than just a necessity.

INTRODUCTION

J ohn Young, when he was the chief executive officer of Hewlett-Packard, once showed one of his customers around an HP facility in the US. The visitor, who was also a competitor to HP in some aspects of its business, was amazed at the openness of HP people. They happily shared technical information and perhaps, more surprisingly, knowledge of the process that HP had, right through from design to manufacture to market. The visitor asked Young why he was not afraid that the visit would impact adversely on HP's competitive position. Young replied that he had no concerns because however much the visitor learnt, he would never be able to copy the manner in which HP implemented its process. That depended on HP's culture, something which had evolved over many years. And that, said Young, no one could imitate.

Nokia is not afraid of showing off to the outside world.

Nokia and HP have a lot in common. In the same manner as HP, Nokia is not afraid of showing off to the outside world. When you listen to Nokia people talking, you get the same impression of eerily unshakeable confidence. Their liking for joint ventures, even ones involving their most dangerous competitors, is fuelled in part, by necessity, as will be demonstrated. But they also welcome joint ventures because, like HP, they believe that the Nokia Way protects their ability to remain leaders in every field.

Nokia has said

"The Mobile Information Society will not be built by any one organisation alone. It requires extensive co-operation between entities which may also be competitors. Such complex collaborations must be managed in an intelligent and enlightened way to ensure that the benefits outweigh the drawbacks. If successful, however, it will mean that together we will break through the limits that restrain progress much faster than we ever could alone."[1]

No Limits

That's nice talk, of course. Many companies speak it, but then again very few act in the way they talk. Here's how Nokia acts in different types of joint venture.

JOINT VENTURES IN TECHNOLOGY

Nokia is in an industry where a certain level of co-operation is beneficial as well as necessary. It is hard not to be impressed with the current far-sightedness of the mobile technology industries when it comes to co-operation. In the old days of mainframe computers, IT users were beset with "compatibility" problems. What this meant, when you boiled it down, was that there were a full 57 different varieties of ways in which one machine might not talk to another. IT competitors developed operating systems and applications packages individually and then used the incompatibilities this caused to lock in their customers to their brand. Back in the seventies, of course, it still required a lot of courage, as well as a lot of investment money, to consider changing your computer supplier.

Perhaps because of the nature of their business – communications – the mobile technology industry takes a totally different approach. Take Wireless Application Protocol (WAP). WAP has been the key to mobile phones becoming mobile information terminals. The aim has been that everyone can download the WAP specification from the Internet and use it to develop applications and services for mobile terminal users. The specification for this technology is code-named "Bluetooth."

The Bluetooth group began with five founder members – Nokia, Ericsson, IBM, Intel and Toshiba – seeking to achieve common standards for WAP. Once there was a common wireless application protocol, the way was then open for devices to talk to each other. Mobile terminals would be able to put devices such as scanners and printers into action. Nokia claims that more than 1000 companies are now committed to making their applications compatible with Bluetooth.

So far so good. Next, application developers needed a common operating system in hand-held devices themselves if they were to offer the market services independent of the hardware devices they use as terminals. Nokia is currently placing its faith in the Symbian joint venture. Symbian is developing an operating system which can be common to a large range of portable devices ranging right through from mobile phones to Personal Digital Assistants (PDAs.) Nokia was an early adopter of Symbian as was Psion (the originator of the operating system) and Ericsson.

Comment on – *Microsoft*
People in the computer industry, in the days when IBM was the dominant supplier, used to say that it was foolish to regard IBM as a competitor. Instead, it was in fact the environment in which they had to compete.

The same could be said of Microsoft, and the big test of Symbian will be its customer's reaction to it and Microsoft's alternative.

The reasons its partners give for working with Nokia can be revealing. In July 2000[2] Cable & Wireless formed a joint agreement with Nokia to develop an Internet platform for mobile phones. The announcement caused great excitement amongst analysts who saw it as a great opportunity for C&W to extend its revenue streams beyond its core focus of providing data, Internet and voice services to businesses. One analyst suggested the revenues could be as much as EUR 850 million. Why were they so keen on Nokia?

Others have said

"Going in with Nokia makes a lot of sense as the standards set for the next generation of mobile services are going to be fragmented and dominated by the big phone manufacturers."[3]

Jim Ross, analyst ABN Amro

And from Cable & Wireless itself:

Nokia has said

"You can see this market's size, it's huge. By combining the strength of our global Internet protocol structure and hosting centres with Nokia's innovative wireless Internet solutions and leading position in the mobile market Cable & Wireless is opening up this new market for its customers."[4]

No Limits

And so the technological co-operation goes on. Most recently the three big players in mobile technology, Nokia, Motorola and

Ericsson founded, in Autumn 2000, a new organization to boost location-based service development. Location-based services are already developing. They allow mobile users to receive services based on their geographic location or position. You can receive local weather forecasts or traffic information, review the menus of local restaurants and find out if any of your friends are in town. The three companies want to combine to push that development further, because they all believe that there is lots to be said for offering a greater range of lifestyle services.

Comment on – core business

The nineties was the decade in which most corporations put "getting back to core businesses" as a key part of their strategy. This reversed the strategy of the eighties where diversification was king. Perhaps the "nought-ies" will be the decade when a balance is struck. Yes, stick to the core business but rely on others to help you take that strategy forwards.

There are already a number of mobile positioning systems in use throughout the world that lack, according to the founder companies, "interoperability" – perhaps the 58th way of describing the ability of one machine to talk to the other. The joint venture is called Location Interoperability Forum (LIF). Its aim is "to produce a common view on positioning technologies and systems solutions to meet the emerging requirements such as information retrieval and mobile commerce applications."[5]

It is therefore easy to see why Nokia loves joint ventures. In this industry, it seems, the markets grow faster because of co-operation: everyone benefits from having the same standards. But there are other reasons why joint ventures are so important to Nokia.

JOINT VENTURES FOR NEW MARKET DEVELOPMENT

Name the two biggest national markets for Nokia in 1999. You probably got the first one, the US. The second was China. On the mobile phones side, Nokia believes that by the end of 2000 there will be some 70 million mobile phone users in China, more than any other country. Using mobile phones is a fantastic possibility for people living in a country with little telecommunications infrastructure. Its an even more fantastic opportunity to those who get in there and sell them to the Chinese.

In May, 2000 Nokia revealed its joint venture strategy in China with the announcement that it was setting up, in partnership with the state owned Capitel Corp, the Xingwang industrial park in Beijing which they hope will become a center for the manufacture and development of telecommunications equipment for China.[6]

Nokia has said

"We have had 10 or 12 other companies potentially interested in investing in the park. We calculated the investment on the basis of 20 companies agreeing to locate there."[7]

Folke Ahlback

The main aim of the park was to persuade Nokia's suppliers to move close to the company's main plant, thereby cutting transport costs. In August 2000, IBM got in on the act. It signed a contract with a Chinese partner to produce electronic components for Nokia in the Xingwang industrial park.

Comment on – *China*

It is rare nowadays for any boardroom not to have the immense opportunity of the Chinese market high on their list of priorities. Many products have had trouble making money. If ever you had to go with the flow and culture of an overseas market, China appears to be the epitome. It seems that you have to engage their people and investment locally.

It's taken many years of patience for Nokia to get to the point of such a joint venture. In order to crack China, Nokia had to show some originality in its approach in the mid-1990s. Nokia has said that it uses China as a manufacturing base to save costs for its global business.[8] In truth, they have also had no alternative but to set up manufacturing facilities there. There are strict regulations in China, making sure that foreign firms bring jobs and expertise to the country, as well selling products into the country. The country sets quotas on imports of telecommunications equipment on Nokia and its competitors and the size of that quota depends on how committed each company is in localizing production. The higher the mainland output, the higher the quota.

Nokia claims to be the first company to bring in GSM technology to mainland China. Their publicity material records that the first GSM phone call was made in Beijing by the Post and Telecommunications Minister in 1994. Nokia's chief representative in China, Folke Ahlback, gives an interesting insight into how Nokia used the demonstration to lead the way into China. The demonstration showed the Chinese government exactly how much of a business opportunity there was in GSM, he says, and adds:

Nokia has said

"Nokia thrives on 'discontinuities' in the market in technologies. It was not absolutely clear at the time that GSM was the standard China would settle on."[9]

Folke Ahlback

Four years later GSM technology dominated the market and Nokia's star in China has risen with it.

Some other joint ventures deal with new ways of selling instead of new places in which to sell. In one foray into the fashion world, Nokia did a deal with the Scandinavian airline SAS to sell its mobile phones through SAS Flightshop, their in-flight sales outlet.

Others have said

"As SAS Flightshop is moving away from a traditional inflight assortment, we are looking for new types of designed products linked to strong brands. The majority of our customers who are travelling for business, appreciate luxurious and trendy products of high quality. Nokia's designed mobile phones fulfil all these requirements."[10]

Rickard Nisell, director SAS Flightshop

JOINT VENTURES FOR RE-ENGINEERING PROCESSES?

This is a less likely area for a joint venture. In early 2000, Nokia formed a joint venture with the IT services group ICL in order to speed up the former's adoption of electronic business. The deal is to build applications that will develop electronic links between Nokia and its resellers and suppliers. The *Financial Times*[11] reported that: "The two concerns have formed a new company to develop Internet applications for Nokia faster than under conventional IT contract agreements." Although mobile sector alliances are common – Ericsson, the rival Swedish manufacturer, has allied with Microsoft to develop consumer wireless e-mail – it is uncommon for an equity deal to focus on a company's internal processes. The new company has been two-thirds owned by ICL with Nokia taking the remaining stake. In the past, ICL has bought Nokia technology to develop mobile Web services for third-party customers.

Others have said

"Now everyone has to develop projects much more quickly. We have formed the new company so that the two of us don't have to waste time with separate negotiations on service agreements. Nokia will be its customer and it will be based in Helsinki to be near to Nokia."[12]

Essa Tihila, director of global business at ICL, a subsidiary of Fujitsu, the Japanese technology company.

Giving your business processes to a partly owned subsidiary company? Surely a good example of the confidence that Nokia believes it gains from the Nokia Way.

ALLIANCES: FOR THE RECORD

The following boxed sections show just some of the major international alliances and co-operation projects that Nokia is involved in.

KEY FACTS

BLUETOOTH SPECIAL INTEREST GROUP (1998)

Nokia, Ericsson, IBM, Intel and Toshiba have together introduced low-cost, short-range radio technology. Enabling seamless voice and data transmission via wireless, short-range radio, this new technology allows users to connect a wide range of devices easily and quickly, without the need for cables, expanding communications capabilities for mobile computers, mobile phones and other mobile devices, both in and out of the office. The specification for this innovative technology, code-named "Bluetooth," is being developed through the combined contributions of the members of the Bluetooth Special Interest Group (SIG). The SIG was formed in early 1998 as a result of the global commitment of the five founding companies to develop the concept towards a technology standard.

GLOBAL MOBILE SUPPLIERS ASSOCIATION (1998)

Formed by Nokia and 20 other founding members from across the telecommunications industry. The organization's key aims include the promotion of GSM products, systems and services in new and existing markets and the promotion of GSM network evolution to support a new generation of services. The GSA also intends to co-operate with, and complement other bodies working in the GSM field.

HIPERLAN2 GLOBAL FORUM (1999)

Nokia, Bosch, Dell, Ericsson, Telia and Texas Instruments formed HiperLAN2 Global Forum, an open industry consortium with the objective to provide common connectivity for mobile communications and to ensure interoperable products are produced under the same standard.

LIFECHART.COM (1999)

A new e-health company LifeChart.com has been formed by combining the technology, personnel, marketing and assets of Nokia's health-related wireless applications business (Wellmate) with Silicon Valley health monitoring company ENACT Health Management Systems. LifeChart.com will combine Nokia's Internet and wireless health management system for diabetes and the personal health monitoring and management system for asthma that was the origin of ENACT.

MOBEY FORUM (2000)

Major financial institutions and the leading mobile phone manufacturers (ABN AMRO Bank, Banco Santander Central Hispano, BNP Paribas, Barclays, Citigroup, Deutsche Bank, HSBC Holdings, MeritaNordbanken, SEB-Skandinaviska Enskilda Banken, UBS, Visa International, Ericsson, Motorola and Nokia) announced the creation of a global forum to encourage the use of mobile technology in financial services and to drive the adoption of open standards in this field.

MOBILE ELECTRONIC TRANSACTIONS INITIATIVE (2000)

Nokia, Ericsson and Motorola announced a joint effort to develop an open and common industry framework to secure mobile electronic transactions. The target of this initiative is to use existing and emerging standards to build a common framework and to create an implementation roadmap in order to enhance the fast adoption of trusted mobile e-business.

OXYGEN ALLIANCE (2000)

Acer Group, Delta Electronics, Inc., Hewlett-Packard Company, Nippon Telegraph and Telephone Corporation, Nokia Research Center, and Philips Research, will work with MIT researchers to create a new breed of pervasive, human-centered computers devoted to serving people's needs.

SYNCML INITIATIVE (2000)

Nokia, IBM, Lotus, Motorola, Nokia, Palm, Inc., Psion and Starfish Software founded the SyncML initiative to develop and promote an industry specification for data synchronization of remote data and personal information across multiple networks, platforms and devices.

WAP FORUM (1998)

A new company, Wireless Application Protocol Forum Ltd. (WAP Forum), was established by Ericsson, Motorola, Nokia and Unwired Planet (now Phone.com). This non-profit company administers the worldwide WAP specification process and facilitates new companies contributing to WAP specification work. The Wireless Application Protocol (WAP) is targeted to bring Internet content and advanced services to digital cellular phones and other wireless terminals.

WIRELESS LAN ALLIANCE (WLANA)

Nokia joined WLANA, an educational trade association for the wireless local area networking industry. Other members include 3Com Corporation, Aironet Wireless Communications, Inc., Breeze-Com. Inc., Cabletron Systems, Inc., Harris Semiconductor, Intermec Technologies, Lucen Technologies, Nortel Networks Wireless LAN Group and Symbol Technologies, Inc.

3G.IP (1999)

Nokia, AT&T, BT, Rogers Cantel, Ericsson, Lucent Technologies, Nortel Networks, Telenor and TIM are forming a 3G.IP focus group to develop an all IP-based architecture for new types of mobile systems.

ASK YOURSELF

Here are the five points that Nokia tends to get right. How well does your organization do?

1 Thinks about joint ventures and alliances in terms of the longer term development of the market.
2 Makes sure that joint ventures are carried out in an open fashion.
3 Does whatever it takes to crack new markets. Joint ventures can be a tool with which to achieve this or a result of it.
4 Is not afraid to use a joint venture for any purpose, even to re-engineer itself.
5 Does not allow a joint venture to adversely affect its chances for market leadership.

NOTES

1   *No Limits*, Nokia 2000.

2   The *Guardian*, 2000.

3   See note 2.

4   See note 1.

5   Nokia, Motorola, Ericsson press release, 2000.

6   *Financial Times*, 2000.

7   The *South China Post*, 1998.

8   See note 7.

9   See note 7.

10   See note 5.

11   See note 6.

12   See note 2.

Nine

NEVER FORGET THAT BOTTOM LINE

Nokia spends a ton of money on research and development, design and marketing, but it has a reputation amongst its staff for being rather stingy. This chapter looks at the whether Nokia's financial results are as good as the preceding chapters suggest they should be. Of all the matters that have gone before, what are the key financial elements that produce success for the bottom line?

At the risk of mixing clichés, the proof of the pudding is in the bottom line. We have discussed the Nokia Way and tried to unravel the secrets that has made the company such a dominant power in the field of mobile technology. But do the financial results that Nokia has achieved in the past merit the praise heaped on the company? After all, success in business is ultimately defined in terms of making money.

Everyone knows that Nokia makes a lot of money, but it is doing so in a rapidly expanding market. To make realistic assessment of financial performance you need a benchmark. The one this book has chosen is Nokia's arch rival in Scandinavia, Ericsson. The Swedish mobile phone giant still has sales revenues considerably in excess of Nokia. First though, it pays to look first at the shape of finance you need to run a thriving, growing company in the telecommunications field.

NOKIA'S R&D AND THE BOTTOM LINE

What high demands does a mobile technology company face on its cashflow? Nokia as a manufacturer has a requirement for large capital investment which, in 1999, amounted to 1.3 billion Euro, nearly 7 percent of sales. Mobile technology companies have to be seen to be spending a lot of money on research and development. And to ensure that it stays ahead of the game with the seemingly shortening life cycles of products, investment in R&D has also had a considerable impact on the resources of a company. In 1999, Nokia employed more than 17,000 people in R&D in 52 centers across 14 countries. R&D as a percentage of sales, is one of only two ratios where Ericsson seems to have an advantage.

All the following comparative numbers are calculated from the two companies' annual reports to December 1999.

All currency numbers in EURm	Nokia 1999	Nokia 1998	Ericsson 1999	Ericsson 1998
R&D spend	1,755	1,150	3,354	2,982
R&D spend as a %age of sales	8.8%	8.6%	13.2%	13.7%

Commentators seem to have little concern about this, and indeed they openly express their opinion that Nokia will continue to win the new product battle. The experts believe, though not unanimously, that each of Nokia's competitors may spend more on R&D, but waste a lot of money when it comes to management processes and the way they develop and launch new products.

Others have said – *handsets*

"Nokia is aggressively pursuing market share growth objectives ... to achieve this they are expecting to take advantage of weaknesses in several key competitors (caused by both supply management and product launch issues) and are aggressively cutting selling price across all platforms through their brand in traditionally slow months."[1]

Others have said – *infrastructure*

"We expect that continued emphasis on financing and a strong balance sheet will be needed to support 3G, (third generation) roll-outs for which spectrum is currently being auctioned across Europe."

Deutsche Banc Alex. Brown, Equity Research, 2000

So why are the commentators so confident?

NOKIA'S EMPLOYEES AND THE BOTTOM LINE

One answer seems to be that Nokia manages to get more out of its employees for the money it spends on them. The company's operating efficiency ratios are a good measure of how a company's business processes can make a big difference to profitability. From what has been written before in this book and taking into account that the Nokia Way is the much-vaunted basic pillar on which the company is built, we should expect to see a good performance.

[Nokia] has a reputation among some of its staff for being a little on the stingy side for such a profitable company ...

Then we come to the employee ratios, and the only people Nokia seems to disappoint are its own employees. It has a reputation among some of its staff for being a little on the stingy side for such a profitable company and the average wage per employee relative to Ericsson suggests that this view has merit. This is the only other figure where Nokia appears to be inferior to Ericsson, and then only if you happen to work for them. Note that these figures are not in millions but in round Euros.

All currency numbers in EUR	Nokia 1999	Nokia 1998	Ericsson 1999	Ericsson 1998
Sales per employee	386,345	324,305	242,941	215,152
Profit per employee	75,131	59,770	19,052	22,206
Average wage per employee	38,025	39,108	41,807	37,593

It is perhaps important though to bear in mind that the employee comparisons, while not exactly comparing oranges with bananas need to be treated with at least a little caution. The geographic spread of employees makes a difference to the workers (workers obviously tend to be cheaper in less developed parts of the world) as do the relative skill sets of the workforce. But if you care to jump to a conclusion based on these figures you might say that the Nokia Way makes the company an attractive one to work for, and that at least some of the employees agree to earn less than they otherwise might.

INVENTORY, PAYMENT AND THE BOTTOM LINE

Take two other main indicators, stock turnover and collection periods. The first of these measures how effective the company is in making what it needs to meet orders and deliver them quickly. In other words, "How many times per year does the company completely sell out its stock." The second measures the time it takes a company to get money in from its customers.

	Nokia 1999	Nokia 1998	Ericsson 1999	Ericsson 1998
Stock turnover	11.2	10.3	8.4	6.8
Collection period in days	70.6	76.9	107.7	106.7

FINANCING AND THE BOTTOM LINE

A look at the balance sheet shows just how strong it is. A company of Nokia's size often needs to get hold of a lot of money at very short notice. Global acquisition opportunities in the telecommunications world come very expensive and often happen with next to no notice, so the company needs to have the ability to be fast on its financial feet and, if necessary, have access to borrowings if it needs them. This is made easier by its current AAA rating that the financial ratings agency Dun and Bradstreet[2] have awarded the company – the highest rating it can award.

Despite its growth, Nokia's interest-bearing liabilities have stayed much the same today as they were in 1995.

Ease of financing is one aspect of the Nokia story. A lack of long-term debt is another. Despite its growth, Nokia's interest-bearing liabilities have stayed much the same today as they were in 1995. With long-term debt at 0.4 billion EUR and shareholders funds at 7.4 billion EUR the company could hardly be in a stronger position to convince others that it has the ability to take advantage of investment opportunities as they arise.

Comment on – *gearing*

A huge number of companies in the technology industry are struggling with too little capital. Borrowing is not a long-term solution for most, so they need to search out other sources of capital. It is becoming increasingly difficult to do this with a lot of venture capitalists waiting to see before risking any more money in the sector.

A comparison of gearing ratios with those for Ericsson is informative. The company's capital gearing ratio is a comparison of a company's long-term debt with its shareholders funds. The higher the ratio, the more likely it is that debt could become a difficult burden. Income gearing is the ratio of interest payable to the profits out of which interest is paid. This latter ratio is often taken as the most important gearing ratio nowadays since it is impossible to fudge in the annual report.

	Nokia 1999	Nokia 1998	Ericsson 1999	Ericsson 1998
Capital gearing	16.2%	22.0%	62.1%	33.9%
Income ratio	6.2%	7.5%	15.0%	11.5%

In both cases the companies are strong, but Nokia is stronger by some distance. In addition, Ericsson's gearing ratios have increased markedly while Nokia's have fallen away in spite of its phenomenal growth.

LIFE ON THE BOTTOM LINE

Comment on – *staff efficiency*

Most managers use their resources more efficiently if they have to prove the need for them in financial terms. This means estimating gains and losses that will emerge from the additional costs, and having some measures of productivity.

Now let's look at those all-important profit margins. When a product achieves the kind of global demand that all the main players in the mobile technology are enjoying at the moment, you might expect a squeeze on margins, with prices discounted to maintain market share. Despite Nokia's emphasis on personalization for the customer, mobile phones look increasingly like a utility bought on price.

In chasing market share, an avowed strategy of the company – according to Morgan Stanley, who make these points – Nokia takes some risk with its margins.

Others have said

"One message that came over clearly in a recent conference call and in our conversations with the company is that Nokia is determined to prioritise market share ... The lack of new phones in Q3 to drive higher average selling prices (ASP's) has meant that Nokia has had to pursue market share aggressively to drive revenues. This has hurt margins – partly because of the lower percentage of higher-ASP phones, and partly because, to maximise market share, the company needs to focus on volumes at the low end of the market."[3]

Nokia has its other product divisions, of course, particularly Nokia Networks, but even this business-to-business product range faces healthy competition and pressure on margins as well. The key measure of all this are the gross margin, and the operating margin. Jorma Ollila, in Nokia's 1999 report and accounts, says that operating margin is well above the industry average. Given the figures below, it is difficult to argue with him.

All currency numbers in EURm	Nokia 1999	Nokia 1998	Ericsson 1999	Ericsson 1998
Sales	19,772	13,326	25,500	21,835
Cost of goods sold	12,227	8,299	14,902	12,460
Gross margin	61.8%	61.3%	41.6%	42.9%
Operating profit	3,908	2,489	2,082	2,282
Operating margin	19.8%	18.7%	8.2%	10.6%

Unlike a lot of its partners and competitors in the mobile technology industry, Nokia pays out a significant amount of its profits in dividends. Its age and its importance for the health of the Finnish economy means that its shares are held not only as a growth stock, but also for dividend income this year. The yield at the time of writing is a measly 0.4 percent, showing that the market expects the company to continue its rapid growth thus allowing the dividend to grow strongly in the future.

In the end, dividends and R&D are paid out of bottom line profits, and the Nokia record on this front is excellent.

All currency numbers in EURm	Nokia 1999	Nokia 1998	Ericsson 1999	Ericsson 1998
Sales	19,772	13,326	25,500	21,835
Profit before tax	3,845	2,456	1,999.8	2,253.6
Profit margin	19.4%	18.4%	7.8%	10.3%
Return on capital employed	48.6%	44.0%	14.2%	18.9%

EVERY SILVER LINING HAS A CLOUD

All that has gone before in this book attempts to explain how Nokia achieves the first-class financial performance outlined in this chapter. Nokia's culture has directly produced excellent results for a number of years. But the views of the analysts may give us some clues about their concerns for the future. Morgan Stanley Dean Witter actually downgraded its ratings for Nokia in mid-2000, albeit a downgrade from Strong Buy to Outperform. This means that they still expect Nokia to outperform its industry sector average, and the market generally.

The firm gives three reasons for the downgrade. The first of these is Nokia as a victim of its own past success. They predicted that Q3, 2000, would show a quarter-on-quarter decline in earnings per share for the first time since 1995, a prediction that turned out not to be true.

According to a press release dated October 19th 2000, sales in Q3 rose by 50 percent and profits by 39 percent

The second issue is whether Nokia's enviable track record for executing its plans, and knowing its customer base well enough to make accurate predictions, can be maintained.

Others have said

"Nokia's execution seems to have slipped. The key explanation for the company's lower-than-expected forecast Q3 Mobile Phones margin seems to be that Nokia will have a lower proportion of new, and therefore higher-margin phones than anticipated previously. Moreover, the company said it has chosen to put market share ahead of margins. We think this may be more than a Q3 issue."[4]
Morgan Stanley Dean Witter, European Investment Perspectives, 2000

Their third concern is the rate of growth in the handset industry. This has been phenomenal over the last few years, and at some point analysts are aware that rate of growth will slow down. The huge growth rates that have fuelled Nokia's performance might be becoming a thing of the past.

But in the end, there is still a consensus that Nokia is about to exploit a window of opportunity this year in relation to its competing with Motorola and Ericsson. Here is the argument.

Others have said

"Whether a short- or long-term strategy, we think Nokia may have spotted an opportunity to increase its market share this year. Its biggest competitors, Motorola and Ericsson have both made strategic decisions to put profitability before market share, and we do not believe either of them have any significant new products ... The supply constraints that would have prevented Nokia from pursuing this strategy ... seem to be easing, and may ease first for Nokia, given that is the industry leader and an efficient supply-chain manager."[5]

Morgan Stanley Dean Witter, European Investment Perspectives, 2000

WALKING THE FINANCIAL TIGHTROPE

Nokia managers spend the company's money as though it is their own. They have a reputation for a tight control of costs. Yet they are prepared to sanction often far-out and lateral R&D projects. It may sound like Nokia managers need referring for schizophrenia, yet theirs is a superb balancing act, borne out of the knowledge throughout the company of what it is trying to achieve.

> Nokia managers spend the company's money as though it is their own.

Comment on – *managers' spending*

Managers who are trying to get their people to spend money as if it were their own should use the rule of 2 percent. This says that if your figures all get worse by just 2 percent, that is sales down and costs up, then the overall impact on the bottom line is actually 46 percent drop in profitability. If, on the other hand, you can make all your figures improve by just 2 percent this has the overall effect of improving results by the same margin.

For a company doing so well, finance is not, or at least has not been since the difficult days of the early nineties, a major constraint on the thought processes of the business. Tight control of costs has a role, but more as an underpinning discipline than as a kill-joy override. The bottom line is always there, however, and no one can forget it. The financial scorecards sitting on the intranet, monitoring all aspects of performance, make sure of that.

ASK YOURSELF

Here are the five points that Nokia tends to get right when it comes to getting results on the bottom line. How well does your organization do?

1 They are well capitalized with a low amount of debt.

2 Their operating efficiencies show how well they use their employees.

3 Their employees are more efficient because they know why they are doing something.

4 Nokia managers remain stingy when it comes to controlling costs.

5 Nokia managers don't confuse overall cost control with risk aversion.

NOTES

1   Deutsche Banc Alex. Brown, Equity Research, 2000.

2   Business Information Report, Dun and Bradstreet, 2000.

3   Morgan Stanley Dean Witter, European Investment Perspectives, 2000.

4   See note 3.

5   See note 3.

---◆---

Ten

LEARN FROM THE PAST AND PREPARE FOR THE FUTURE: WILL NOKIA CONTINUE TO BE SUCCESSFUL?

---◆---

This chapter draws the lessons of the other chapters together. In particular it looks at recent question marks over whether Nokia can continue its run of success.

GOOD THINGS CAN'T GO ON FOREVER, CAN THEY?

At the beginning of August 2000, and again in January 2001, some elements of the media suddenly suggested Nokia's aura of invincibility had been shattered. For example the *Financial Times*' Lex Column noted that:

Others have said

"Delays in new product launches will result in the margins on mobile phones shrinking from 25 per cent in the second quarter to somewhere in the mid teens in the third quarter. Problems with one new model could be put down to bad luck. But Nokia is behind schedule on several. This casts doubt on its ability to execute better than its rivals – which Nokia must if it is to stay ahead of the pack and maintain mobile phone margins above 20 per cent in the future."

Lex Column, 1 August, 2000

The announcement of the delays in August caused Nokia shares to plunge more than 20 percent in a single day. In absolute terms this meant $51.9bn being wiped off the company's value, thought to be the largest ever single-day loss at that time by a European company.

The skeptics were wrong. Third-quarter figures once again exceeded market and media expectations. And a month later the company introduced another breakthrough product, the Nokia 9210 Communicator, the first Nokia product to make use of Symbian (the new technology platform that gets more out of mobile terminals such as communicators and smart phones).

The recent developments were a salutary lesson in long-term perspective. Nokia has ridden the upwave of phenomenal growth in demand for mobile technology. This has meant that over five years, from 1995–1999, sales figures have trebled, and profits have increased fivefold. But during this time, Nokia has also given a sixfold increase in dividends.

Yet in spite of all this, analysts do still have concerns for the future. Morgan Stanley Dean Witter, for example, actually downgraded its ratings for Nokia in mid-2000, albeit a downgrade from Strong Buy to Outperform. This means that they still expect Nokia to outperform its industry sector average, and the market generally. Worries center around whether is Nokia's enviable track record for executing its plans, and knowing its customer base well enough to make accurate predictions, can be maintained. The second concern is the rate of growth in the mobile handset industry. This has been phenomenal over the last few years, and at some point analysts are aware that rate of growth will slow down. The huge growth rates that have fuelled Nokia's performance might be becoming a thing of the past.

The disappointment is understandable. Investors had seen Nokia as a special case – a magical company which seemed to

beat even the highest expectations time after time. By definition, however, even top-notch companies will disappoint from
time to time. If you are a football team that wins 5–0 every
week and is top of the league, 4–0 or second place is a bit of a
let down. Even results matching expectations can disappoint
money markets that have become thoroughly spoilt on good
news.

Others have said

"It eventually becomes a self-defeating cycle, because you can't keep
exceeding expectations when the expectations are so high."

Susan Anthony, analyst at Credit Lyonnais Securities

The mark of true greatness for any company is not that it manages to constantly exceed expectations, because expectations
never stand still. Rather it is that it is able to ignore short-term
adversity and keep the markets happy over the long term by
having the correct processes in place to deliver good long-term
results.

The skeptics certainly have a point. Nokia certainly has issues
to face not only in delayed product launches but also in the
area of component shortages and market saturation in some
parts of the world. And even without these, there's a relentless development of new technologies over which Nokia must
dominate, along with an increasingly complex relationship
with mobile operators as the third-generation mobile services
unfold.

Nokia, in common with any company, will suffer many reverses
in the future when dealing with such difficult issues, but it is
the nature of its reaction to adversity that really counts. And

throughout this book, the company has shown signs of being able to adapt in the face of adversity since it was born. The seeds of the modern Nokia were only sown in the 1980s even though the company is 135 years old. Until then, Nokia was a messy, disorganized conglomerate struggling to survive. Yet, as we have seen, telecommunications and mobile phones have gone from 10 percent of sales to the entire business in a market of phenomenal growth. That's some reaction to adversity.

You could argue that Nokia has had the good fortune to be in the right market at the right time. It's a fair point, but it doesn't explain how the company has managed to recover a few times from adversity in the 1990s – and consistently beat the pants off the opposition. And since 1995, Nokia has enjoyed twice the growth in stock price of its Scandinavian rival Ericsson and ten times that of the US giant Motorola. Even if you think that Nokia got lucky being in a rapidly expanding market, it's difficult to put those kinds of differences down to plain old good fortune. There must be things going on inside the company and in the way it deals with the outside world which have been intrinsically superior to the best efforts of the rest.

...
since 1995, Nokia has enjoyed twice the growth in stock price of its Scandinavian rival Ericsson and ten times that of the US giant Motorola.

So what are these "things?" Well, as we have seen, it's about leadership for starters. Understanding what Nokia people mean by leadership is absolutely crucial to understanding what makes the company work. Leadership isn't just about having a strong personality at the helm – although in Jorma Ollila they certainly have one – but comes through setting down clear policies to achieve objectives, even radically brave ones, which everyone throughout the company understands.

Leadership and bravery are twin pillars on which so much of Nokia's success is built. At the start of the 1990s, Nokia put in place some clear objectives. Like many other companies at the time, it wanted to ditch its unwieldy conglomerate image. Unlike many others, however, it focused with some bravery on what many at the time considered its non-core operations – and sold off its core activities. To understand how brave a decision that was, you have to remember that, at that time, the company had been teetering on the edge of bankruptcy and the global economy was in chaos. It was by no means obvious that Nokia should be any more a "focused" electronics firm than a "focused" rubber company. Many experts believed that Nokia should focus on neither, but should instead protect itself by diversifying further.

> Leadership and bravery are twin pillars on which so much of Nokia's success is built.

Nokia's philosophy on bravery revolves around the elimination of the idea that anyone at the company should be afraid of failure. Fear of failure breeds mediocrity. The company's blame-free culture keeps people trying all manner of innovative approaches in order to keep the Nokia company ahead of the game. Bravery is therefore tied in with a freedom to act. Nokia people are encouraged to have a go and so the sense of bravery gets translated further down the organization.

It is Nokia practice to announce a strategy change to a group of individuals and then for that group immediately to consult with the next level down on the implications of the change for them. What this means is that everybody recognizes that they have some involvement in the way in which the company is managed. This recognizes that at the end of the day decisions have to be sometimes made rapidly owing to the nature of the business. In short, leadership at Nokia breeds efficient performance. Any conversation with somebody from Nokia will give you a real feeling that everyone – from leader to new recruit, without exception – knows what the company is trying to achieve and their part in that process. And for as long as this remains the case, that has to bode well for future performance.

Many companies say that they value the people who work for them … Most, in reality, run themselves on the high-octane fuel of fear.

Putting respect for the individual at the heart of this strategy in this way is important, but how to make it work in practice? Many companies say that they value the people who work for them, but few have such a well-documented statement of their people strategy. Most, in reality, run themselves on the high-octane fuel of fear. They organize themselves in terms of their people, put command and control at the heart of their policy, with little genuine respect for employee involvement and participation.

Part of the answer lies in structure. Flatter structures mean a much higher involvement of everyone with the running of the business. Nokia's structure itself is as flat as a pancake. This flat structure is a necessary (though not sufficient, as many others have discovered) condition for the way in which Nokia handles its staff. Nokia insists that its employees should work to specific and measurable objectives, not least because staff have a right to know exactly what is expected of them. This is much easier to invoke in a flatter structure. Also, everyone knows how everyone else is doing. This is because the company's key performance indicators are all set up on the company's intranet. There is little sign, in spite of the rapid recruitment, that the company structure is becoming bloated and hierarchical.

> ... it's not just about whether a candidate can do a particular job, but whether he of she can do it within a rapidly changing environment.

Certainly, recruiting good staff quickly can be a nightmare. All HR areas are important to business success, but this area has been critical to Nokia's continued success. It's not easy to recruit sometimes, with so many other things going on as the company develops. And for Nokia, it's not just about whether a candidate can do a particular job, but whether he of she can do it within a rapidly changing environment. Nokia overcomes this problem because they're not just looking for people who understand the technology but also for people who can apply the company's values and not just worry about how they fit into the company's hierarchy.

Fortunately, in terms of the future, the success of Nokia's brand has undoubtedly been helpful in recruitment, as has the company's obvious sense of spirit. Keeping hold of staff is at least as challenging, and hence staff motivation is also a key issue. Many companies offer share options to quality staff as a cheap and cash-free way of keeping them interested in the fortunes of the company and Nokia has its own incentivising employee share-option schemes. The expansion of the market is a major incentive in keeping people with Nokia. The company has no particular hierarchy and so, in a fast-growing atmosphere, you have to move people around to get experience of different parts of the business. As long as the company has done its job in recruiting the right sorts of people at an early stage, then new challenges and responsibility are the greatest forms of motivation. But if the market stops growing rapidly, staff retention may yet become a major problem for Nokia over the longer term.

To ensure that the market doesn't stop growing, Nokia has proved itself adept at meeting the needs of its customers – and anticipating their future needs. Nokia's ability to focus on their bottom-line wants is an increasingly crucial part of any business. Nokia does this by thinking about customer lifestyles. Lifestyles are changing very fast – and a large part of Nokia's efforts is geared to anticipating changes in consumer psychology when making a purchasing decision.

Of course what people want is different depending on who you are talking to. These days, there is no single entity known as "the market" when it comes to mobile technologies. Instead there are whole load of micro-markets aimed at particular varieties of wants and needs and the only certainty is that there will be more variety, not less, in the future. There is no mobile phone that will serve everybody's needs. The aim instead is that everybody finds a mobile phone for their personal needs and wants. Nokia has to oblige this sophistication because customers are now more ruthless than ever. Current success is always fickle in such circumstances. Nokia works on retaining its customers by appealing to them as a company that will always have the latest thinking on a new market segment – before any of its competitors. This means, in turn, that Nokia has to be sufficiently ruthless at an early stage of research and development about which products to keep – and which to dispense with.

Another reason to be optimistic about the future of Nokia is its brand value – incredibly important in this day and age. The brand is something that Nokia has been working on really, really hard and single mindedly since the early 1990s. This investment now seems to have paid off. The most recent survey from marketing consultants, Interbrand, shows that Nokia was the fifth most-recognized brand in the world, after Coca-Cola, Microsoft Windows, IBM and Intel. That's no mean achievement from a company that only began to go wholeheartedly into the mobile telecommunications market in 1992.

There are other reasons for hope that Nokia can react well to adversity. It has a good track in reacting well in the past. As we have also seen, innovation is never ending to Nokia and is not just limited to the products and services provided to the customer. When the company had a huge distribution bottleneck in the mid-1990s, how did the company react? Well, no one got blamed for a start. Instead everyone at the company was made aware of what was going on and was encouraged to look at their own potential contribution to the solution, whether they worked in distribution or not. This was no patch-work solution, but a complete review of the company's overall distribution strategy which, via a taskforce and the consequent swift introduction of new logistics, soon evaporated.

Nokia also treats its suppliers with considerable respect – the company's respect for the individual extends to the way it deals with its business partners. It sets out the values it requires of its partners and then leaves the rest to them, because it believes that those business partners are the best judges of how to implement the values. There is no doubt that Nokia pushes its suppliers hard, but is loyal to those who meet its requirements. Customers are calling the shots as manufacturers scramble to meet their needs, so Nokia expects their suppliers to be as dedicated to innovation as they are.

Nokia's treatment of suppliers extends to its approach to joint ventures. There are very many reasons why companies join joint ventures and alliances, and Nokia is an enthusiastic advocate of all of them. Nokia's leaders see joint ventures and alliances as a thoroughly desirable fact of life rather than just a necessity. This is partly because it is in an emerging industry where a certain level of co-operation is beneficial as well as necessary because of the needs to adopt fresh standards and protocols. Nokia also gets involved in joint ventures in order to develop new markets.

Coming round full circle to Nokia's financial results, it is worth taking a good look at the composition of the company's balance sheet. A company of Nokia's size needs to get hold of a lot of money at short notice and its credit rating is first class, as is its lack of long-term debt and its low gearing ratio. The company spends a ton of money on research and development and design and marketing, but it has a reputation for tight control of costs. Nokia somehow gets more out of its employees for the money it spends on them. The company has an inferior average wage per employee relative to its chief rival, Ericsson, one of the few financial indicators in which the Swedish company is superior. Even so, a look at the overall balance sheet shows just how strong Nokia is.

In spite of these possible clouds on the horizon, there is little doubt that Nokia is still the company that the others want to beat. It understands the consumer market better than its rivals and spends more on research, giving it a technology edge in the market. The company's economies of scale are unmatched. This in turn helps to ensure that it has the best access to components.

INDEX

INDEX